First Settlers

in

Georgia

Volume 7

Abstracts of English Crown Grants
in
St. Andrew Parish, 1755–1775

Evans, Liberty, Long, McIntosh, and Tattnall Counties

Pat Bryan

Surveyor General Department
State of Georgia

Heritage Books
2024

HERITAGE BOOKS
AN IMPRINT OF HERITAGE BOOKS, INC.

Books, CDs, and more—Worldwide

For our listing of thousands of titles see our website
at
www.HeritageBooks.com

A Facsimile Reprint
Published 2024 by
HERITAGE BOOKS, INC.
Publishing Division
5810 Ruatan Street
Berwyn Heights, MD 20740

Originally Printed 1972
by the State Printing Office
Atlanta, Georgia

Reprinted by Special Permission of
Georgia State Archives
1998

International Standard Book Number
Paperbound: 978-0-7884-2791-6

Introduction

The Royal Charter of June, 1732, given by King George II to
the Trustees for Establishing the Colony of Georgia in America,
defined the boundaries of the new colony as lying between the
Savannah and Altamaha Rivers, extending as far north as those
rivers flowed and thence from their sources in a straight line
to the South Seas.

The land in question was in possession of the Creek and Cherokee
Nations, and when James Edward Oglethorpe, one of the Trustees
and the leader of the colony, landed at Yamacraw Bluff on the
Savannah River on February 12, 1733, he was well aware that
some agreement with the Indians was necessary. His first treaty
with the Creeks in 1733 assured him of a small area along the
Savannah River, running north along it to a point opposite
today's Rincon, passing through that town and today's Eden in
a diagonal line to the Ogeechee, thence south and a little
west in a straight line to the Altamaha River, or, as it has
been described elsewhere, "the area between the Savannah and
the Altamaha as high as the tides flowed." This was the small
part of the original charter grant in which the colonists settled and here they laid out the City of Savannah.

The 1733 Treaty with the Creeks reserved two parcels of land
for themselves. One was an area from Pipemaker's Bluff to
Palachucolas Creek and the other was the Islands of Ossabaw,
Sapelo, and St. Catherine. It was not until 1757 at a congress
held as Savannah that a treaty between the English and the
Creeks gave to Georgia the three great Sea Islands and the
small tract of land in reserve near Savannah. By this time,
too, the colonists had settled considerably beyond the limits
of the first treaty and came to look upon all this land as
their own. Oglethorpe had early fortified St. Simons Island
knowing well that it was outside of the treaty boundary as
well as the charter limits. The next year in 1758, without
treaty or permissions from the Indians, an Act of the Assembly
created seven parishes, i.e., St. Paul, St. George, St. Matthew, Chrish Church, St. Philip, St. John and St. Andrew.
By Royal Proclamation in 1763, the English Crown extended
Georgia's southern boundary to the St. Marys River, and by
Act of Assembly again, the four new parishes of St. David,
St. Patrick, St. Thomas and St. Mary were created from that
extension in 1765.

The Creeks were uneasy about these expansions and in order to
quiet them and to redefine the western boundary, a new treaty

Introduction

was made in 1763 at Augusta. The limits of the settlers went as far as the Little River to the north, down the Ogeechee to the southwest corner of the present boundary line of Bulloch County, southward crossing the upper reaches of the Canoochee River and ended at the St. Marys.

The last of the Royal Provincial treaties was in 1773 and this included what was called the Ceded Lands, a rich area acquired from the Creeks and Cherokees north of the Little River to the Broad and west almost to the Oconee River. Settlement in this area was barely begun when the first fires of the Revolution were seen in the Province and until that war was over, Georgia remained a relatively narrow strip along the Savannah to the Ogeechee River.

Under the Trustees, from 1732 until the charter was resigned to the Crown in 1752, all allottments or leases of land made to the settlers were in Tail Male. Unlike fee simple grants, the leases could not be mortgaged, sold or otherwise disposed with. Some confusion exists about these allottments and leases, since some of the written records refer to them as grants, when, strictly speaking, that term is not correct. In 1752, after the relinquishment of the charter, Georgia became a Royal Province and under the English Crown and its Royal Governors, fee simple grants were made to the land which gave a clear title to the grantees. These Royal Grants, in the Georgia Surveyor General Department of the Office of the Secretary of State, begin in 1755. The three year gap between 1752 and 1755 is variously explained by historians, but in any case, the latter year is the first date for the grants. There are some 5000 of these recorded.

The department has now abstracted, very carefully and accurately, all of the Royal Provincial Grants. Using cards, citations to survey date, grant date, acres, name of grantee, page and book of record are shown, and a verbatim extraction of the description of the property granted. The legal verbiage of "Appurtenances and hereditaments" has been omitted. All else is shown in the abstract.

During the Revolution, according to one of the state's early Surveyors General, many of the plats of survey for the Royal Grants were destroyed. In abstracting the grants, it was found that only one grant in four had the plat of survey. Also, some plats existed for which there was no grant issued, although there were not many of these. In the text, where the reader

Introduction

finds no citation for a survey, there is none, and, conversely,
where no grant is shown, there is none extant.

It is hoped that this effort will give important data to state
officials first, and then to geographers, historians and the
general public.

Transition from Districts and Towns into
Parishes in 1758 and 1765 to Counties in 1777

1732 - 1758 Districts & Towns	1758 - 1765 Parishes	1765 - 1777 Parishes	1777 Counties
District of Augusta	St. Paul	St. Paul	Richmond
District of Halifax	St. George	St. George	Burke
District of Abercorn	St. Matthew	St. Matthew	Effingham
District of Goshen	St. Matthew	St. Matthew	Effingham
District of Ebenezer	St. Matthew	St. Matthew	Effingham
District of Ogechee (above Canoochee River)	St. Philip	St. Philip	Effingham
District of Ogechee (below Canoochee River)	St. Philip	St. Philip	Chatham
Town of Hardwick	St. Philip	St. Philip	Chatham
Town of Savannah	Christ Church	Christ Church	Chatham
District of Savannah	Christ Church	Christ Church	Chatham
Sea Islands north of Great Ogechee River	Christ Church	Christ Church	Chatham
Town of Sunbury	St. John	St. John	Liberty
District of Midway	St. John	St. John	Liberty
District of Newport	St. John	St. John	Liberty
St. Catherines Island	St. John	St. John	Liberty
Bermuda Island	St. John	St. John	Liberty
Town of Darien	St. Andrew	St. Andrew	Liberty
District of Darien	St. Andrew	St. Andrew	Liberty
Sapelo Island	St. Andrew	St. Andrew	Liberty
Eastwood Island	St. Andrew	St. Andrew	Liberty
Sea Islands between Great Ogechee & Altamaha Rivers	St. Andrew	St. Andrew	Liberty
Town of Frederica	St. James	St. James	Liberty
District of Frederica	St. James	St. James	Liberty
Great St. Simons Island	St. James	St. James	Liberty
Little St. Simons Island	St. James	St. James	Liberty
Sea Islands south of Altamaha River	St. James	St. James	Liberty
Between Altamaha & Turtle River		St. David	Glynn
Between Turtle and Little Satilla Rivers		St. Patrick	Glynn
Between Little Satilla & Great Satilla Rivers		St. Thomas	Camden
Between Great Satilla & St. Marys River		St. Mary	Camden

Horatio Marbury & William H. Crawford. Digest of the Laws of Georgia (Savannah 1802) P. 150-153.

State of Georgia. 1777 Constitution, Section 242.

Anderson, David
200 acres in St. Andrews Parish

Granted on December 5, 1769   Grant Book G, page 486

200 acres bounded on the north by the said David Anderson,
east by Charles West and on the west by Thomas Quarterman.

****

Anderson, David
100 acres in St. Andrew Parish

Granted on May 7, 1771   Grant Book I, page 304

100 acres bounded on the north by William Jones, east by
Joseph Bacon, south by land purchased by the said grantee
from Joseph Goodby.

****

Andrew, Benjamin
150 acres in St. Andrew Parish

Granted on January 19, 1773   Grant Book I, page 842

150 acres bounded on the north by the said grantee and on
all other sides by vacant land.

****

Andrew, Benjamin
150 acres in St. Andrew Parish

Granted on July 5, 1774   Grant Book M, page 4

150 acres bounded on the northwest by the said Benjamin
Andrew and on all other sides by vacant land.

****

Andrew, James
150 acres in St. Andrew Parish

Granted on November 1, 1768   Grant Book G, page 206

150 acres bounded on the east by James Andrew and on all
other sides by vacant land.

Andrew, Joseph
300 acres in St. Andrew Parish

Surveyed on June 17, 1760   Plat Book C, page 3
Granted on May 21, 1762   Grant Book D, page 109

****

Andrew, Joseph
150 acres in St. Andrew Parish

Granted on March 1, 1763   Grant Book D, page 285

150 acres bounded on the south by Moses Way and John Martin
and on all other sides by vacant land.

****

Arthur, Francis
300 acres in St. Andrew Parish

Granted on February 1, 1763   Grant Book D, page 278

300 acres bounded on the east by John Martin and on all other
sides by vacant land.

****

Arthur, Francis
150 acres in St. Andrew Parish

Granted on February 1, 1763   Grant Book D, page 279

150 acres bounded on the south by John Martin, east by Joseph
Andrew and north by John Baker.

****

Arthur, Francis
100 acres in St. Andrew Parish

Granted on February 1, 1763   Grant Book D, page 280

100 acres bounded on the north by John Martin and on all
other sides by vacant land.

Ashmore, Strong
150 acres in St. Andrew Parish

Granted on July 7, 1761   Grant Book I, page 700

150 acres bounded on the north by Francis Arthur, east by
Barach Norman, south by Thomas Christie and Richard Baker.

****

Askins, John
350 acres in St. Andrew Parish

Granted on March 2, 1773   Grant Book I, page 909

350 acres bounded on the south by the Altamaha River, east
by John Clark and on all other sides by vacant land.

****

Bacon, John
200 acres in St. Andrew Parish

Granted on February 7, 1775   Grant Book M, page 976

200 acres bounded on the northeast by Benjamin Farley, on
the north by unknown land and on the northwest by John Stuart.

****

Bacon, Jonathon
150 acres in St. Andrew Parish

Granted on April 7, 1772   Grant Book I, page 545

150 acres bounded on all sides by vacant land.

****

Bacon, Thomas
300 acres in St. Andrew Parish

Granted on February 7, 1775   Grant Book M, page 984

300 acres bounded on the southwest by Hannah Bradwell and on
the northeast by Abraham Lewis.

Bacon, William
250 acres in St. Andrew Parish

Granted on April 7, 1772   Grant Book I, page 543

250 acres bounded on all sides by vacant land.

                              ****

Bacon, William
300 acres in St. Andrew Parish

Granted on April 7, 1772   Grant Book I, page 544

300 acres bounded on all sides by vacant land.

                              ****

Bacon, William
150 acres in St. Andrews Parish

Granted on October 4, 1774   Grant Book M, page 419

150 acres bounded on the southwest and northeast by William
Bacon.

                              ****

Bacon, William
100 acres in St. Andrew Parish

Granted on February 7, 1775   Grant Book M, page 975

100 acres bounded on the southeast by Stephen Williams, north
by David Anderson, east by William LeConte and south by Daniel
Sullivant.

                              ****

Bailey, Robert
500 acres in St. Andrew Parish

Granted on February 3, 1762   Grant Book D, page 49

500 acres bounded on the south by the Altamaha River, north
by Cathead Creek and northeast by William Mackay.

Baillie, Alexander
150 acres in St. Andrew Parish

Granted on July 5, 1774   Grant Book M, page 5

150 acres bounded on the southeast by Angus Clark, northeast
by Ann McIntosh and northwest by John Rian and Edmund Hammond.

****

Baillie, Alexander
100 acres in St. Andrew Parish

Granted on April 4, 1775   Grant Book M, page 1094

100 acres bounded on all sides by vacant land.

****

Baillie, George
182 acres in St. Andrew Parish

Granted October 4, 1774   Grant Book M, page 418

182 acres bounded on the south by John Gray, southeast by
George McIntosh, northeast by Roderick McLeod and northwest
by land run for John Gray and by land of George McIntosh.

****

Baillie, Kenneth
500 acres in St. Andrew Parish

Granted on July 7, 1761   Grant Book C, page 75

500 acres bounded on the east by William Gibbons and on all
other sides by vacant land.

****

Baillie, Robert
50 acres in St. Andrew Parish

Granted on November 6, 1764   Grant Book E, page 59

50 acres bounded on the north by John Grant, east by Hugh
Ross and west by Samuel Fulton.

Baillie, Robert
200 acres in St. Andrew Parish

Granted on January 6, 1767   Grant Book F, page 13

200 acres bounded on the south by John Wetherspoon and on all
other sides by vacant land.

****

Baillie, Robert
1000 acres in St. Andrew Parish

Granted on November 3, 1767   Grant Book F, page 401

1000 acres bounded on the northwest by Burgon Bird, John
Mackay and the Sapelo River, and on the northeast by land
laid out for John Jagger,

****

Baillie, Robert
150 acres in St. Andrew Parish

Granted on September 6, 1768   Grant Book G, page 171

150 acres bounded on the southeast by Ann McKintosh and on
all other sides by vacant land.

****

Baillie, Robert
400 acres in St. Andrew Parish

Granted on November 7, 1769   Grant Book G, page 453

400 acres bounded on the southwest by the said Robert Baillie
and on all other sides by vacant land.

****

Baillie, Robert
150 acres in St. Andrew Parish

Granted on June 2, 1772   Grant Book I, page 621

150 acres bounded on the west by John McDonald and John
Ponshare and on the northwest by Ann McIntosh.

Baillie, Robert
600 acres in St. Andrew Parish

Granted on November 1, 1774   Grant Book M, page 621

600 acres bounded on the north by George McIntosh, John
McDonald and vacant land, and northwest and southwest by
Robert Baillie.

****

Baillie, Robert
500 acres in St. Andrew Parish

Surveyed on December 28, 1760   Plat Book C, page 17

500 acres bounded on the north by the Altamaha River.

****

Baker, Edward
100 acres in St. Andrew Parish

Granted on May 4, 1773   Grant Book I, page 967

100 acres bounded on the west by land of an old survey and
on the northeast by South Newport River and salt marsh.

****

Baker, Edward
300 acres in St. Andrew Parish

Granted on June 7, 1774   Grant Book I, page 1060

300 acres bounded on the south by Alexander McDonald, east
by land supposed to be surveyed for some person unknown.

****

Baker, John
300 acres in St. Andrew Parish

Granted on April 13, 1761   Grant Book C, page 134

300 acres bounded on the northwest by Samuel Jeanes and on all
other sides by vacant land.

Baker, John, Jr.
100 acres in St. Andrew Parish

Granted on December 6, 1768   Grant Book G, page 225

100 acres in St. Andrew Parish bounded on all sides by vacant land.

****

Baker, Joseph
150 acres in St. Andrew Parish

Granted on September 5, 1769   Grant Book G, page 406

150 acres bounded on the south and east by Thomas Mackay and on the northwest by Moses Way.

****

Baker, Joseph
300 acres in St. Andrew Parish

Granted on June 2, 1772   Grant Book I, page 631

300 acres bounded on the northwest by Greis Elliott, partly on the southeast by William Peacock and on all other sides by vacant land.

****

Baker, Richard
200 acres in St. Andrew Parish

Granted on October 4, 1768   Grant Book G, page 193

200 acres bounded on the west by Henry Petty, north by Richard Baker and east by Thomas Quarterman.

****

Baker, Richard
245 acres in St. Andrew Parish

Granted on July 7, 1772   Grant Book I, page 656

245 acres bounded on the south by the Altamaha River, east by Rutherfords Creek, north by Lewis Creek and west by a creek called the thoroughfare. In trust.

8

Baker, Richard
300 in St. Andrew Parish

Grant on December 7, 1762   Grant Book D, page 260

300 acres granted Richard Baker in trust for Joseph and
Thomas Stevens and bounded on all sides by vacant land.

****

Bannister, Ann
130 acres in St. Andrew Parish

Granted on January 3, 1775   Grant Book M, page 846

130 acres bounded on the southwest by Button Gwinnett, south
east by William Bannister and northeast by John Potson.

****

Barber, John
250 acres in St. Andrew Parish

Granted on August 4, 1767   Grant Book F, page 309

250 acres bounded on the north partly by John Jones and partly
by land vacant, south partly by Roderick McIntosh and partly
by land vacant and on the northwest by the Newport River.

****

Barfield, Henry
150 acres in St. Andrew Parish

Granted on July 4, 1769   Grant Book G, page 353

150 acres bounded on the northeast by John Grey, southwest by
Lachlan McKintosh and northeast by Donald Kennedy.

****

Barnaby, John
100 acres in St. Andrew Parish

Granted on July 7, 1767   Grant Book F, page 285

100 acres bounded on the south by the Sapelo River and on the
east by Robert Johnson.

9

Barnaby, John
150 acres in St. Andrew Parish

Granted on January 2, 1770   Grant Book G, page 492

150 acres bounded on the south by a branch of the Sapelo River
and west by the said John Barnaby.

****

Bates, Thomas
200 acres in St. Andrew Parish

Granted on May 15, 1756   Grant Book A, page 219

200 acres bounded on the northeast by John Jagger and near
the Sapelo River.

****

Bennett, Hugh
200 acres in St. Andrew Parish

Granted on May 5, 1772   Grant Book I, page 580

200 acres bounded on the west by Peter Grant and John Martin.

****

Bennett, William
150 acres in St. Andrew Parish

Granted October 2, 1770   Grant Book I, page 168

150 acres bounded on all sides by vacant land.

****

Bennett, William
150 acres in St. Andrew Parish

Granted on March 5, 1771   Grant Book I, page 263

150 acres bounded on the southwest by land of the said grantee.

****

Bord, Burgon
400 acres in St. Andrew Parish

Surveyed on November 4, 1760   Plat Book C, page 18
Granted on February 3, 1762   Grant Book D, page 30

400 acres bounded on the southeast by Captain John McIntosh
and on the southwest by John McKay.

****

Bosomworth, Thomas
500 acres in St. Andrew Parish

Granted on July 5, 1774   Grant Book M, page 9

500 acres bounded on all sides by vacant land.

****

Bourguin, Henry
255 acres in St. Andrew Parish

Surveyed on May 4, 1758   Plat Book C, page 16

255 acres on the north side of Sappalo River bounded on the
west by land formerly allotted Robert Johnson and on all other
sides by marshes and a creek.

****

Bourguin, Jane
350 acres in St. Andrew Parish

Granted on June 2, 1772   Grant Book I, page 645

350 acres bounded on the north by William Spencer.

****

Bowman, John
600 acres in St. Andrew Parish

Granted on May 5, 1772   Grant Book I, page 579

600 acres in St. Andrew Parish including 200 acres being the
surplus land in a tract purchased by the grantee at Cat Head

Creek and bounded on the north by Lachlan McIntosh and
land purchased by the said grantee of one Westley, west by
Sir Patrick Houston, south by Cat Head Creek and land
granted Angus McKay now also belonging to the said grantee.

****

Bowman, John
750 acres in St. Andrew Parish

Granted on September 6, 1774   Grant Book M, page 291

750 acres bounded on the south by the said John Bowman and
by John Stacey.

****

Bowman, John
750 acres in St. Andrew Parish

Granted on September 6, 1774   Grant Book M, page 292

750 acres bounded on the south by John Stacey and Edmund
Pierce.

****

Bowman, John
700 acres in St. Andrew Parish

Granted on November 1, 1774   Grant Book M, page 632

700 acres bounded on the north by North Branch of the Altamaha
River, south and east by the south and east branches of the
Altamaha River and west by John Hume.

****

Bradford, John
250 acres in St. Andrew Parish

Granted on September 1, 1767   Grant Book F, page 339

250 acres bounded on the west by land formerly ordered Robert
Johnson and on every other side by a creek and marhses leading
from Sapelo River, which said tract was heretofore ordered to
Henry Bourguin.

Bradshaw, John
250 acres in St. Andrew Parish

Granted on November 3, 1767   Grant Book F, page 400

250 acres bounded on the east by Daniel Ross and on all other sides by vacant land.

****

Bradwell, Hannah
500 acres in St. Andrew Parish

Granted on October 1, 1771   Grant Book I, page 425

500 acres bounded on all sides by vacant land.

****

Bradwell, Hannah
300 acres in St. Andrew Parish

Granted on February 4, 1772   Grant Book I, page 507

300 acres bounded on the east by the said grantee and on all other sides by vacant land.

****

Brown, Francis
150 acres in St. Andrew Parish

Granted on July 5, 1774   Grant Book M, page 10

150 acres bounded on the east by Sheets land on all other sides by vacant land.

****

Bryan, Jonathon
900 acres in St. Andrew or St. John Parish

Granted on July 4, 1758   Grant Book A, page 652

900 acres, Broughtons Island in the Altamaha River, 760 acres of which are marsh land and 140 acres of which are river swamp.

****

Bryan, Jonathon
83 acres in St. Andrew Parish

Granted on August 7, 1759   Grant Book B, page 378

83 acres bounded on the north by the 5 acre lots of Darien and south by the Altamaha River, including an island called Doboy.

****

Burton, Elizabeth
150 acres in St. Andrew Parish

Granted on July 1, 1760   Grant Book B, page 502

150 acres bounded on the east by the said Robert Burton, husband of Elizabeth, north by John Quarterman and southeast by Stephen Williams.

****

Butler, James
500 acres in St. Andrew Parish

Granted on January 3, 1775   Grant Book M, page 844

500 acres bounded on the southeast by Noble Jones and vacant land and on the northwest by Teleman Cuyler.

****

Butler, Joseph
100 acres in St. Andrew Parish

Granted on July 4, 1769   Grant Book G, page 349

100 acres bounded on all sides by vacant land.

****

Calwell, Henry
450 acres in St. Andrew Parish

Granted on August 7, 1759   Grant Book D, page 333

450 acres bounded on the northeast by vacant land and on all other sides by creeks and marshes of Sapelo River.

Camber, Thomas
450 acres in St. Andrew Parish

Surveyed on March 28, 1760   Plat Book C, page 34
Granted on May 21, 1762   Grant Book D, page 78

450 acres being part of an island bounded on the south by
Crooked Creek, west by land vacant and on every other side
by the River Altamaha.

****

Camber, Thomas
450 acres in St. Andrew Parish

Surveyed on March 18, 1760   Plat Book C, page 34
Granted on May 21, 1762   Grant Book D, page 79

450 acres bounded by a creek. The original warrant (q.v.)
states that the land is located upon a neck between Darien
and Sapelo River.

****

Cameron, Alexander
100 acres in St. Andrew Parish

Surveyed on November 1, 1759   Plat Book C, page 33

100 acres located at Cherry Tree Bluff on South Newport River
adjoining David Douglass on the west, according to the original
warrant. (q.v.)

****

Cammeron, Alexander
100 acres in St. Andrew Parish

Granted on May 1, 1759   Grant Book B, page 72

100 acres bounded on the north by South Newport River marshes,
southeast by Stephen Dickinson and southwest by Sir Patrick
Houstoun.

****

Cantey, James
300 acres in St. Andrew Parish

Granted on October 1, 1771   Grant Book I, page 428

300 acres bounded on the southwest by the Altamaha River
and on the northeast by John Jamieson, John Jones and land
laid out for the use of the dissenting clergyman.

****

Cantey, James
200 acres in St. Andrew Parish

Granted on May 5, 1772   Grant Book I, page 581

200 acres bounded partly on the west by John Jones and part
vacant, south by George Davis, east by Witherspoon, north by
old surveyed land and on all other sides by vacant land.

****

Carr, Mark
220 acres in St. Andrew Parish

Surveyed on June 24, 1761   Plat Book C, page 33
Granted on May 21, 1762   Grant Book D, page 84

220 acres situate and being an island bounded on the northeast
by the River Altamaha called South River opposite Governor
Wright's Great Island, northwest by the Altamaha River called
Back River opposite Governor Wright's Little Island and on
the south by Fishing Creek. Plat states that this tract is
also bounded by New Hanover.

****

Carter, Thomas
100 acres in St. Andrew Parish

Surveyed on October 2, 1761   Plat Book C, page 33
Granted on May 21, 1762   Grant Book D, page 106

100 acres bounded on the southwest by the Altamaha River and
on all other sides by vacant land.

****

Christie, Thomas
100 acres in St. Andrew Parish

Surveyed on February 14, 1760   Plat Book C, page 35

100 acres bounded on the north by John McPherson, east by
Curtis other land, south by William Miles and John Quarterman.
Original warrant state (q.v.) that land is located at Bear
Head Swamp on the South Branch of the North Newport River.

****

Christie, Thomas
350 acres in St. Andrew Parish

Granted on July 7, 1761   Grant Book D, page 3

350 acres bounded on the west by Richard Baker and on the
south by John Sertain and William Mills.

****

Clark, Angus
500 acres in St. Andrew Parish

G^Ranted on October 2, 1759   Grant Book B, page 198

500 acres bounded on all sides by vacant land.

****

Clark, Angus
100 acres in St. Andrew Parish

Granted on March 6, 1770   Grant Book G, page 542

100 acres bounded on the southeast by Edmund Hammond and on
the northeast by John Rian.

****

Clark, Hugh
500 acres in St. Andrew Parish

Granted on February 11, 1757   Grant Book A, page 306

500 acres bounded on the northeast by the Sapelo River and
on all other sides by vacant land.

Clark, Hugh
200 acres in St. Andrew Parish

Surveyed on April 15, 1760   Plat Book C, page 35
Granted on July 7, 1761   Grant Book C, page 132

200 acres bounded on the northwest by Mackenzie and Bales and
on all other sides by vacant land.

****

Clark, John
300 acres in St. Andrew Parish

Granted on June 7, 1774   Grant Book I, page 1046

300 acres bounded on the south by the Altamaha River and on
the west by land laid out for John Askins.

****

Clark, Nathaniel
200 acres in St. Andrew Parish

Granted on February 7, 1758   Grant Book A, page 638

200 acres bounded on the north by Captain James McKay and
on the south by White Outerbridge.

****

Clark, Stephen
250 acres in St. Andrew Parish

Surveyed on July 10, 1759   Plat Book C, page 34
Granted on April 3, 1764   Grant Book D, page 405

250 acres bounded on the south by Phillippa Fenny, deceased
and north by Stephen Clark. Plat shows that this tract is
bounded on the west by Francis Arthur.

****

Clark, William
500 acres in St. Andrew Parish

Granted on February 11, 1757   Grant Book A, page 307

500 acres bounded on the east by the Sapelo River.

Clark, William
200 acres in St. Andrew Parish

Granted on January 3, 1775   Grant Book M, page 862

200 acres bounded on the northwest by Robert McKay.

****

Clarke, Donald
500 acres in St. Andrew Parish

Granted on March 28, 1758   Grant Book A, page 590

500 acres bounded on all sides by vacant land.

****

Clarke, James
100 acres in St. Andrew Parish

Granted on March 6, 1770   Grant Book G, page 541

100 acres bounded on the northeast by John McDonald and on all
other sides by vacant land.

****

Cooper, Richard
200 acres in St. Andrew Parish

Granted on January 3, 1775   Grant Book M, page 860

200 acres bounded on the southeast by _____Whitter, southwest
by John Bacon, northwest by Baker and Joseph Way and northeast
by _____Gibbons.

****

Cox, Thomas
300 acres in St. Andrew Parish

Surveyed on February 28, 1760   Plat Book C, page 33
Granted on January 4, 1763   Grant Book D, page 273

300 acres bounded on the west by John Baker and on the south
by William Davis.

****

Crighton, Alexander
200 acres in St. Andrew Parish

Granted on January 3, 1775   Grant Book M, page 856

200 acres bounded on the northeast by John Wynn and on all other sides by vacant land.

****

Curtis, John
103 acres in St. Andrew Parish

Surveyed on June 8, 1761   Plat Book C, page 34

103 acres bounded on all sides by vacant land.

****

Curtis, John
200 acres in St. Andrew Parish

Granted on November 1, 1774   Grant Book M, page 634

200 acres bounded on the northeast by John Winn and on all other sides by vacant land.

****

Cuyler, Telamon
500 acres in St. Andrew Parish

Granted on October 1, 1771   Grant Book I, page 427

500 acres bounded on all sides by vacant land.

****

Cuyler, Telemon
400 acres in St. Andrew Parish

Granted on January 7, 1772   Grant Book I, page 489

400 acres bounded on the southwest by the Altamaha River and James Woroland and east by Sherrard.

****

Davies, George
200 acres in St. Andrew Parish

Granted on April 30, 1761   Grant Book C, page 37

200 acres bounded on all sides by vacant land.

                    ****

Davis, William
350 acres in St. Andrew Parish

Granted on July 1, 1760   Grant Book B, page 528

350 acres bounded on the east by Thomas Smith and on all
other sides by vacant land.

                    ****

Davis, William
200 acres in St. Andrew Parish

Surveyed on April 30, 1757   Plat Book C, page 54

200 acres bounded on the north by Duglass, south by salt
marsh and west by the said William Davis.

                    ****

DeBrahe, Christopher

150 acres in St. Andrew Parish

Granted on March 7, 1769   Grant Book G, page 276

150 acres on Wolf Island bounded on the west by a creek and
salt marsh and on the east by sea beach.

                    ****

Delegal, David
54 acres in St. Andrew Parish

Granted on November 5, 1771   Grant Book H, page 61

54 acres bounded on the northwest by salt marsh, east by
John Jones and south by John Barber.

                    ****

Delegall, David
300 acres in St. Andrew Parish

Granted on December 3, 1771   Grant Book I, page 472

300 acres bounded on the west by South Newport River, south
by Roderick McIntosh, east by salt marsh, north by Barber and
lands said to belong to Roderick McIntosh.

****

Demere, Raymond
100 acres in St. Andrew Parish

Granted on April 7, 1772   Grant Book I, page 549

100 acres bounded on the northeast by John Perkins and on all
other sides by vacant land.

****

Demetre, Daniel
500 acres in St. Andrew Parish

Granted on May 15, 1756   Grant Book A, page 120

500 acres bounded on the north by said Daniel Demetre and
on all other sides by creeks and marshes of Sapelo River.

****

Demetre, Daniel
400 acres in St. Andrew Parish

Granted on May 15, 1756   Grant Book A, page 121

400 acres on an island in the Sapelo River bounded on the
northeast by the Sapelo River, south by land formerly belonging
to John Smith and on all other sides by marshes.

****

Demetre, Daniel
200 acres in St. Andrew Parish

Granted on February 7, 1758   Grant Book A, page 643

200 acres bounded on the east by William Thomas Harris, southwest by marshes of South Newport River.

****

Demetre, Daniel
50 acres in St. Andrew Parish

Granted on February 7, 1758   Grant Book A, page 644

50 acres on Dickinsons Neck and bounded on all sides by vacant land.

****

Dickinson, Stephen
200 acres in St. Andrew Parish

Granted on December 6, 1757   Grant Book A, page 515

200 acres bounded on all sides by vacant land.

****

Donham, Daniel
250 acres in St. Andrew Parish

Granted on February 5, 1760   Grant Book C, page 285

250 acres bounded on the north and east by James McKay and on all other sides by vacant land.

****

Donnam, James
300 acres in St. Andrew Parish

Surveyed on October 11, 1759   Plat Book C, page 54

300 acres bounded on the north by Outerbridge and vacant land, east by William Gibbons, south by John DeHonneurs and vacant land.

****

Douglass, James
300 acres in St. Andrew Parish

Granted on July 3, 1770   Grant Book I, page 47

300 acres bounded on the southwest by the Altamaha River,
northwest by William McCormack and northeast by Robert
Miller.

****

Drayton, Stephen
300 acres in St. Andrew Parish

Granted on June 7, 1774   Grant Book I, page 1035

300 acres bounded on the north by the said Stephen Drayton,
southeast by Allan and Ann Stuart.

****

Drayton, Stephen
300 acres in St. Andrew Parish

Granted on June 7, 1774   Grant Book I, page 1036

300 acres bounded on the southeast by Allan and Ann Stuart.

****

Dunham, William
300 acres in St. Andrew Parish

Granted on November 6, 1764   Grant Book E, page 60

300 acres bounded on the north by White Outerbridge and
vacant land, east by William Gibbons, south by land laid out
for John Dehonneur and vacant land, and on the west by land
vacant.

****

Earle, John
100 acres in St. Andrew Parish

Surveyed on August 26, 1760   Plat Book C, page 58

100 acres bounded on the south by Broton Island, north by an
island owned by Alexander McKeithene.

Earle, John
100 acres in St. Andrew Parish

Surveyed on November 17, 1760   Plat Book C, page 59

100 acres bounded on the north by Alexander McKethen. The original warrant (q.v.) states that the land was located between Darien and Sapelo near lands granted James Woodland.

****

Elliott, Grey
9520 acres in St. Andrew Parish

Granted on October 31, 1760   Grant Book B, page 495

9520 acres being all those islands called Sapelo and being on the sea coast and bounded on the east and southeast by the Ocean, southwest by a north branch of the Altamaha River and west by a creek called Tea Kettle and the marshes thereof. The grant states that this island is in St. John Parish but Marbury and Crawford's Digest of the Laws of Georgia, 1755-1800 states that it was in St. Andrew Parish. The original warrant (q.v.) states that the islands were surveyed for Grey Elliott September 30, 1760 and the original plat of survey is filed in the maps cases in the Georgia Surveyor General Department.

****

Elliott, Grey
500 acres in St. Andrew Parish

Surveyed on December 2, 1760   Plat Book C, page 58
Granted on November 3, 1761   Grant Book C, page 262

500 acres bounded on the northwest by Charles West, on the northeast by William Elliott and on the south and east by Francis Lee and James McKay.

****

Elliott, Grey
250 acres in St. Andrew Parish

Granted on March 6, 1770   Grant Book G, page 546

250 acres bounded on the southwest by James Read and on the northeast by Samuel Miller.

****

Elliott, Grey
302 acres in St. Andrew Parish

Granted on July 5, 1774   Grant Book M, page 28

302 acres bounded on the north by _____Andrew, east by land
surveyed for Francis Arthur, south by James Cochran, west
by _____James, the same being a surplus found on a resurvey
of land originally surveyed for Francis Arthur, deceased.

****

Elliott, Grey
300 acres in St. Andrew Parish

Granted on July 5, 1774   Grant Book M, page 29

300 acres bounded on the south by the said Grey Elliott.
Seventy-seven acres of the above three hundred being surplus
land contained in an original tract of Grey Elliott.

****

Elliott, Grey and Gordon, John
150 acres in St. Andrew Parish

Granted on April 6, 1773   Grant Book I, page 946

150 acres bounded on the north by Daniel McIntosh and on all
other sides by vacant land.

****

Elliott, Grey and Gordon, John
100 acres in St. Andrew Parish

Granted on August 6, 1765   Grant Book E, page 197

100 acres surveyed for Alexander Cameron and by (him) mortgaged
to Elliott and Gordon; bounded on the south by marshes of
the South Newport River and on the west by land of the late
David Douglass, deceased.

****

Elliott, Grey and Gordon, John
300 acres in St. Andrew Parish

Granted on August 6, 1765   Grant Book E, page 198

300 acres formerly laid out for Samuel Richardson and by him mortgaged to Elliott and Gordon; bounded on the east by Ann Andrew and north by James Andrew.

****

Elliott, Grey and Gordon, John
300 acres in St. Andrew Parish

Survey date not given   Plat Book C, page 299
Granted on August 6, 1765   Grant Book E, page 199

300 acres formerly laid out for Robert Stewart and by him mortgaged to Elliott and Gordon; bounded on the northwest by South Newport River.

****

Elliott, Grey and Gordon, John
150 acres in St. Andrew Parish

Granted on August 6, 1765   Grant Book E, page 200

150 acres formerly laid out for Donald Kenedy and by him mortgaged to Elliott and Gordon; bounded on the northeast by George McDonald.

****

Elliott, Grey and Gordon, John
250 acres in St. Andrew Parish

Granted on March 3, 1767   Grant Book F, page 107

250 acres bounded on the southeast by Samuel Tomlinson and on all other sides by vacant land.

****

Elliott, Grey and Gordon, John
1000 acres in St. Andrew Parish

Granted on March 6, 1770   Grant Book G, page 544

1000 acres bounded on the northeast by said grantees and on the northwest by Daniel McIntosh, and on all other sides by vacant land.

****

Elliott, Grey and Gordon, John
500 acres in St. Andrew Parish

Granted on March 6, 1770   Grant Book G, page 545

500 acres bounded on the north by Robert Stewart and on all
other sides by vacant land.

                              ****

Ewen, William
200 acres in St. Andrew Parish

Granted on September 6, 1774   Grant Book M, page 307

200 acres bounded on the southeast by James McKay, southwest
by James Read, northwest by Samuel Miller and northeast by
vacant land.

                              ****

Farley, Benjamin
150 acres in St. Andrew Parish

Granted on July 1, 1760   Grant Book B, page 458

150 acres bounded on the east by the said Benjamin Farley
and on the west by William Gibbons.

                              ****

Farrer, Bartholomew
200 acres in St. Andrew Parish

Surveyed on July 4, 1761   Plat Book C, page 63
Granted on May 21, 1762   Grant Book D, page 131

200 acres bounded on the north by Lewis Creek, west by Isaac
Lewis and on the south by the Altamaha River.

                              ****

Farrow, Bartholomew
100 acres in St. Andrew Parish

Granted on December 1, 1767   Grant Book F, page 419

100 acres bounded on the east by Robert Johnstone, west by John
Fitzgerald, south partly by John Barnaby and all other vacant.

Fitzgerald, John
300 acres in St. Andrew Parish

Granted on August 5, 1766   Grant Book E, page 334

300 acres bounded on the south by marshes of the South Newport River, on the north by land formerly ordered Douglass, and west by William Davis. 200 acres of this tract was formerly ordered William Davis and 100 acres thereof was ordered to William Wright.

****

Fitzpatrick, Francis
200 acres in St. Andrew Parish

Granted on November 1, 1774   Grant Book M, page 655

200 acres bounded on the south by Hannah Bradwell and on all other sides by vacant land.

****

Forbes, Donald
250 acres in St. Andrew Parish

Granted on August 2, 1774   Grant Book M, page 183

250 acres bounded on the southeast by Charles McDonald and Thomas King and on the south by Sir Patrick Houstoun and Murdock McLeod.

****

Forsyth, John
100 acres in St. Andrew Parish

Granted on November 7, 1769   Grant Book G, page 458

100 acres bounded on the southeast by Murdock McLeod and on all other sides by vacant land.

****

Fox, Benjamin
150 acres in St. Andrew Parish

Granted on March 3, 1772   Grant Book I, page 527

150 acres bounded on the northwest by land surveyed for Daniel McKay and on all other sides by vacant land.

****

Fox, John
500 acres in St. Andrew Parish

Granted on October 4, 1774   Grant Book M, page 423

500 acres bounded on all sides by vacant land.

****

Fox, John
500 acres in St. Andrew Parish

Granted on October 4, 1774   Grant Book M, page 434

500 acres bounded on the southeast by Joseph Oswall and all other sides by vacant land.

****

Fraser, Simon
150 acres in St. Andrew Parish

Surveyed on October 12, 1760   Plat Book C, page 61
Granted on February 3, 1762   Grant Book D, page 33

150 acres bounded on the west by Ann McIntosh and southeast by Hugh Morrison.

****

Fredericks, Matthew
1000 acres in St. Andrew Parish

Granted on March 6, 1770   Grant Book G, page 547

1000 acres bounded on the northwest by Alexander Sharood and vacant land and on the southwest by the Altamaha River.

****

Fulton, David
500 acres in St. Andrew Parish

Surveyed on February 29, 1760   Plat Book C, page 61

500 acres bounded on the east by Samuel Fulton, north by
Isaac Lines and west by James McClelan.

****

Fulton, Paul
100 acres in St. Andrew Parish

Granted on September 1, 1767   Grant Book F, page 343

100 acres bounded on the east by a creek and salt marshes,
north by William Clark and south by James Woodland.

****

Fulton, Paul
150 acres in St. Andrew Parish

Granted on November 6, 1770   Grant Book I, page 179

150 acres bounded on the south by land of said grantee, east
by land of McLelland and west by David Weatherspoon.

****

Fulton, Paul
100 acres in St. Andrew Parish

Granted on November 6, 1770   Grant Book I, page 181

100 acres bounded on all sides by vacant land.

****

Fulton, Samuel
500 acres in St. Andrew Parish

Surveyed on February 28, 1760   Plat Book C, page 60
Granted on February 3, 1762   Grant Book D, page 23

500 acres bounded on the north by Cathead Creek, east by
John McCullock, south by the said Samuel Fulton and west by
David Fulton.

****

Fulton, Samuel
400 acres in St. Andrew Parish

Survey date not given   Plat Book C, page 60
Granted on February 3, 1762   Grant Book D, page 24

31

400 acres bounded on the southwest by David Witherspoon, south by John McCleand and east by James McCleand.

****

Fulton, Samuel
500 acres in St. Andrew Parish

Surveyed on February 28, 1760   Plat Book C, page 60
Granted on May 21, 1762   Grant Book D, page 80

500 acres bounded on the south by Lewis Creek, east by John McCulloch, north by the said Samuel Fulton and David Fulton and west by John Lewis.

****

Fulton, Samuel
74 acres in St. Andrew Parish

Granted on January 5, 1768   Grant Book H, page 1

74 acres bounded on the north by John Grant, west and south by the said Samuel Fulton and on the east by Isaac Lyons and _____Tielson.

****

Fulton, Samuel
350 acres in St. Andrew Parish

Granted on March 2, 1773   Grant Book I, page 915

350 acres bounded on the south by ___Lions, west by Mary McCleland and on the east by John Grant and Peter Nephew.

****

Fulton, Samuel
350 acres in St. Andrew Parish

Granted on December 6, 1774   Grant Book M, page 790

350 acres bounded on the west by Lachlan McIntosh and George McDonald, east by John Weatherspoon, William Bennett and vacant land and on the south by land of Peter Nephew.

****

Gibbons, Ann, spinster
500 acres in St. Andrew Parish

Granted on March 6, 1770   Grant Book G, page 549

500 acres bounded on all sides by vacant land.

                    ****

Gibbons, Arthur
100 acres in St. Andrew Parish

Surveyed on November 4, 1759   Plat Book C, page 66
Granted on May 21, 1762   Grant Book D, page 135

100 acres bounded on the north by marshes of South Newport
River and on the west by Alexander Cameron.

                    ****

Gibbons, Joseph
200 acres in St. Andrew Parish

April 7, 1767   Grant Book F, page 179

200 acres bounded on the northeast by the said Joseph Gibbons
and Robert Stewart and on the southwest by John Lawson and
Angus McCay.

                    ****

Gibbons, Thomas
1000 acres in St. Andrew Parish

Granted on September 6, 1774   Grant Book M, page 314

1000 acres bounded on all sides by vacant land and issued to
William Gibbons, in trust for Thomas Gibbons, son of Joseph
Gibbons, deceased.

                    ****

Gibbons, William
320 acres in St.Andrew Parish

Granted on October 2, 1764   Grant Book E, page 41

320 acres bounded on the south by William Gibbons and James
Heart, east by Samuel Hastings, west by White Outerbridge and
north by vacant land.

Gibbons, William
1000 acres in St. Andrew Parish

Granted on September 6, 1774   Grant Book M, page 314

1000 acres bounded on all sides by vacant land and granted to William Gibbons in trust for Thomas Gibbons, son of Joseph Gibbons, deceased.

****

Gilman, Edward
150 acres in St. Andrew Parish

Surveyed on June 13, 1759   Plat Book C, page 67

150 acres bounded on all sides by vacant land.

****

Girardeau, John Bohun
100 acres in St. Andrew Parish

Granted on June 7, 1774   Grant Book I, page 1083

100 acres bounded on the northeast by Andrew Maybank and William Peacock.

****

Goffe, Francis
470 acres in St. Andrew Parish

Surveyed on July 27, 1761   Plat Book C, page 66
Granted on May 21, 1762   Grant Book D, page 87

470 acres situate on an island and bounded on the east by land of Thomas Camber, south by Crooked Creek and on every other side by the River Altamaha.

****

Golden, Palmer
500 acres in St. Andrew Parish

Granted on August 7, 1759   Grant Book B, page 439

500 acres bounded on the southeast by Samuel Jean and on all other sides by vacant land.

****

Gordon, John and Grey Elliott
150 acres in St. Andrew Parish

Granted on April 6, 1773   Grant Book I, page 946

150 acres bounded on the north by Daniel McIntosh and on all
other sides by vacant land.

                              ****

Gordon, John and Grey Elliott
100 acres in St. Andrew Parish

Granted on August 6, 1765   Grant Book E, page 197

100 acres bounded on the south by marshes of South Newport
River and west by land of David Douglass, deceased. Surveyed
for AlexanderCameron and by him mortgaged to Elliott and Gordon.

                              ****

Gordon, John and Grey Elliott
300 acres in St. Andrew Parish

Granted on August 6, 1765   Grant Book E, page 198

300 acres bounded on the east by Ann Andrew and north by
James Andrew. Formerly laid out for Samuel Richardson and
by him mortgaged to Elliott and Gordon.

                              ****

Gordon, John and Grey Elliott
300 acres in St. Andrew Parish

Survey date not given   Plat Book C, page 299
Granted on August 6, 1765   Grant Book E, page 199

300 acres bounded on the northwest by South Newport River.
Formerly laid out for Robert Stewart and by him mortgaged to
Elliott and Gordon. Elapsed and recertified to Grey Elliott
and John Gordon on April 3, 1964.

                              ****

Gordon, John and Grey Elliott
150 acres in St. Andrew Parish

Granted on August 6, 1765   Grant Book E, page 200

150 acres bounded on the northeast by George McDonald. Formerly laid out for Donald Kenedy and by him mortgaged to Elliott and Gordon.

****

Gordon, John and Grey Elliott
250 acres in St. Andrew Parish

Granted on March 3, 1767   Grant Book F, page 107

250 acres bounded on the southeast by Samuel Tomlinson and on all other sides by vacant land.

****

Gordon, John and Grey Elliott
1000 acres in St. Andrew Parish

Granted on March 6, 1770   Grant Book G, page 544

1000 acres bounded on the northeast by the said grantees and on the northwest by Daniel McIntosh.

****

Gordon, John and Grey Elliott
500 acres in St. Andrew Parish

Granted on March 6, 1770   Grant Book G, page 545

500 acres bounded on the north by Robert Stewart and on all other sides by vacant land.

****

Graham, John
50 acres in St. Andrew Parish

Granted on May 1, 1770   Grant Book H, page 43

50 acres bounded on the southwest by Cat Head Creek, north by Donald Clark and east by the late Sir Patrick Houstoun.

****

Graham, John
350 acres in St. Andrew Parish

Granted on October 4, 1774   Grant Book M, page 445

350 acres bounded on the north by the Altamaha River, south by John Colwell and William McIntosh and west by William Haney.

****

Grant, Catherine, widow
200 acres in St. Andrew Parish

Granted on January 5, 1768   Grant Book G, page 7

200 acres bounded on the west by Sir Patrick Houstoun, north by Murdock McCloud, northeast by James Monroe. Land was originally ordered to and surveyed for Gilbert Grant, her late husband, deceased. See plat of survey for Gilbert Grant, of record at page 66 of Plat Book C.

****

Grant, Gilbert
100 acres in St. Andrew Parish

Granted on December 4, 1759   Grant Book B, page 482

100 acres bounded on the east by George Threadercroft and on all other sides by vacant land.

****

Grant, Gilbert
200 acres in St. Andrew Parish

Surveyed on January 29, 1761   Plat Book C, page 66

200 acres bounded on the north by Murdoch McCloud, west by Sir Patrick Houston and east by James Munroe. See grant of Catherine Grant at page 7 of Grant Book G, above.

****

Grant, James
100 acres in St. Andrew Parish

Granted on May 4, 1773   Grant Book I, page 976

100 acres bounded on the east by a marsh and on all other sides by vacant land.

****

Grant, John
200 acres in St. Andrew Parish

Granted on August 7, 1759   Grant Book B, page 231

200 acres bounded on the south by George Kid and on all other sides by vacant land.

****

Grant, John
100 acres in St. Andrew Parish

Granted on September 1, 1767   Grant Book F, page 345

100 acres being part of the surplus land, which on a resurvey is found to be contained in the mark lines and bounds of a tract of land heretofore granted the said John Grant for 200 acres bounded on the west vt surplus land, on the east by 200 acres allowed the said John Grant on his grant for 200 acres as aforesaid, on the south by land of George Kidd and on the north by land of Peter Nephew.

****

Grant, Peter
450 acres in St. Andrew Parish

Granted on August 2, 1774   Grant Book M, page 193

450 acres bounded on the south by Lachlan McIntosh, east by Donald Rose and John Witherspoon and on the northeast by George Bradshaw.

****

Grant, Peter
150 acres in St. Andrew Parish

Granted on December 6, 1763   Grant Book D, page 358

150 acres bounded on the southwest by George McDonald and on all other sides by vacant land.

****

Graves, William
250 acres in St. Andrew Parish

Granted on September 6, 1774   Grant Book M, page 317

250 acres bounded on the northeast by Josiah Osgood and Thom Osgood and northwest by Francis Brown.

****

Graves, William
1200 acres in St. Andrew Parish

Granted on January 3, 1775   Grant Book M, page 882

1200 acres bounded on the north by John Winn, Jr. and Thomas Carter, east by Thomas Carter and James Scrives, and John Shave, and Nathan Taylor and James Screven, and on the south by John Baker and John Elliott.

****

Gray, George
500 acres in St. Andrew Parish

Granted on September 5, 1769   Grant Book G, page 411
500 acres bounded on the south by Sapelo River, east by John Gray, north by Lachlan McIntosh and southwest by George McIntosh.

****

Gray, John
500 acres in St. Andrew Parish

Granted on March 5, 1756   Grant Book A, page 101

500 acres bounded on the east by Captain Patrick Southerland, north by vacant land and on all other sides by creeks and marshes of Sapelo River.

****

Gray, John
100 acres in St. Andrew Parish

Granted on October 2, 1759   Grant Book B, page 208

100 acres bounded on the northwest by a creek of the Sapelo River and on all other sides by vacant land.

****

Gray, John
100 acres in St. Andrew Parish

Granted on October 2, 1759   Grant Book B, page 209

100 acres bounded on the south by a creek and land of Hugh
Clarke and on all other sides by vacant land.

****

Gray, John
204 acres in St. Andrew Parish

Granted on October 2, 1759   Grant Book B, page 210

204 acres bounded on the southwest by Angus McIntosh and
north by Robert Homer.

*****

Gray, John
455 acres in St. Andrew Parish

Granted on October 2, 1759   Grant Book B, page 211

455 acres bounded on the east by Boran Creek, north by Angus
McIntosh, George McDonald and Angus Mackay.

****

Gray, John
480 acres in St. Andrew Parish

Granted on October 2, 1759   Grant Book B, page 212

480 acres bounded on the southeast by Sapelo River and the
marshes thereof.

****

Gray, John
500 acres in St. Andrew Parish

Surveyed on September 1, 1761   Plat Book C, page 66

500 acres bounded on the southwest by the Sapelo River,
southeast by John Lawson and northwest by Robert Miller.

****

Gray, Robert
250 acres in St. Andrew Parish

Granted on May 5, 1772   Grant Book I, page 587

250 acres bounded on all sides by vacant land.

****

Gray, Robert
150 acres in St. Andrew Parish

Granted on November 1, 1774   Grant Book M, page 661

150 acres bounded on the southeast by Robert Gray and vacant.

****

Griffin, Matthew
150 acres in St. Andrew Parish

Granted on April 6, 1773   Grant Book I, page 945

150 acres bounded on the east by the said grantee.

****

Grounidge, Margaret
100 acres in St. Andrew Parish

Granted on February 5, 1760   Grant Book B, page 373

100 acres in the district of Darien, bounded on the southwest
by Alex McDonald.

****

Gwinnett, Button
1000 acres in St. Andrew Parish

Surveyed on April 29, 1767   Plat Book C, page 67
Granted on April 6, 1773   Grant Book I, page 947

1000 acres bounded on the west by a creek and marshes of Sapelo
River, southeast by land ordered John Gray, southwest by lands
of Angus McIntosh and southeast by lands ordered John Gray.

****

Gwinnett, Button
500 acres in St. Andrew Parish

Granted on October 4, 1774   Grant Book M, page 450

500 acres bounded on the southeast by Clement Martin, north
by John Johnston and Noble Jones.

****

Haimsworth, Joseph
100 acres in St. Andrew Parish

Granted on August 2, 1774   Grant Book M, page 198

100 acres bounded on the southwest by Robert Burton, northwest
by Thomas Quarterman, northeast by David Anderson and vacant
land and on the south by Daniel Sullivan.

****

Hamer, Michael
300 acres in St. Andrew Parish

Granted on April 7, 1772   Grant Book I, page 557

300 acres bounded on all sides by vacant land.

****

Hammond, Edward
100 acres in St. Andrew Parish

Granted on December 4, 1759   Grant Book B, page 342

100 acres bounded on all sides by vacant land.

****

Harbert, William
250 acres in St. Andrew Parish

Granted on September 3, 1765   Grant Book E, page 232

250 acres bounded on the southwest by Altamaha River, northwest
by William Johnson and southeast by Marmaduke Perry and vacant
land.

****

Harold, Edmund
100 acres in St. Andrew Parish

Granted on May 1, 1759   Grant Book B, page 171

100 acres bounded on the south by Clapboard Creek and on all
other sides by vacant land.

****

Harris, Lewis
300 acres in St. Andrew Parish

Granted on June 7, 1774   Grant Book I, page 1043

300 acres bounded on the east by Raymond Demere and land
laid out for John Perkins.

****

Harris, William Thomas
350 acres in St. Andrew Parish

Granted on February 7, 1758   Grant Book A, page 646

350 acres bounded on the north by John Rutledge, east by
a creek and marshes of the Sapelo River.

****

Hawthorn, Nathaniel
300 acres in St. Andrew Parish

Granted on March 7, 1775   Grant Book M, page 1076

300 acres bounded on the west by Mr. Douglass, south by
White and vacant land, north by marshes of Newport River
and east by vacant marsh.

****

Holms, John
400 acres in St. Andrew Parish

Surveyed on January 6, 1760   Plat Book C, page 118
Granted on February 5, 1760   Grant Book B, page 283

400 acres bounded on the east by the 45 acre lots of
Darien and on the south by Cat Head Creek.

****

Homer, Robert
700 acres in St. Andrew Parish

Surveyed on September 29, 1755   Plat Book C, page 81
Granted on May 15, 1756   Grant Book A, page 229

700 acres bounded on the northeast by a branch of Sapelo
River, west by lands formerly laid out for John Stevens.

****

Houstoun, James
500 acres in St. Andrew Parish

Granted on July 7, 1772   Grant Book I, page 682

500 acres bounded on the north and east by Clement Martin
and south by James Lucend.

****

Houstoun, John
250 acres in St. Andrew Parish

Granted on May 4, 1773   Grant Book I, page 1004

250 acres bounded on the east partly by Nicholas Smith and
partly vacant land, on the north by Hugh Bennett and vacant
land, on the west partly by Hugh Bennett and vacant land and
on the south by an old line unknown.

****

Houstoun, John
300 acres in St. Andrew Parish

Granted on June 7, 1774   Grant Book I, page 1015

300 acres bounded on the east by land surveyed for Mrs.
Minis, southwest by land surveyed for Charles McDonald and
James Westley and on the northwest by land surveyed for
John Grant and Nicholas Smith.

****

Houstoun, John
200 acres in St. Andrew Parish

Granted on June 7, 1774   Grant Book I, page 1016

200 acres bounded on the south by John Grant, Nicholas Smith
and the meeting house, east by land surveyed for George
Threadcroft and on the north and west partly by John McDonald
and John McBean and vacant land.

****

Houstoun, John
405 acres in St. Andrew Parish

Granted on August 2, 1774   Grant Book M, page 199

405 acres being the surplus of 2 tracts, one of 200 acres,
originally granted Thomas Threadcraft, the surplus of which
is 180¼ acres and the other tract, granted to Abigail Minis
for 500 acres, the surplus of which is 224 3/4 acres and
all bounded on the northeast by William McIntosh and on the
south by John Houstoun and Robert McKay.

****

Houstoun, John
350 acres in St. Andrew Parish

Granted on August 2, 1774   Grant Book M, page 200

350 acres bounded on the east by John Houstoun, north by
Clement Martin and vacant land and on the southwest by John
Houstoun.

****

Houstoun, Sir Patrick
1000 acres in St. Andrew Parish

Granted on June 7, 1757   Grant Book A, page 466

1000 acres bounded on the south by Cat Head Creek and on the
west by Daniel Clark, and on all other sides by vacant land.

****

Houstoun, Sir Patrick
50 acres in St. Andrew Parish

Granted on August 2, 1774   Grant Book H, page 121

50 acres bounded on the northwest by Lachlan McIntosh,
southwest by Thomas King and southeast by the said Sir
Patrick Houstoun.

****

Houstoun, Sir Patrick
150 acres in St. Andrew Parish

Granted on May 5, 1772   Grant Book I, page 590

150 acres bounded on the north by Thomas King, northeast
by Greenage and on all other sides by vacant land.

****

Houstoun, Sir Patrick
100 acres in St. Andrew Parish

Granted on May 5, 1772   Grant Book I, page 591

100 acres bounded on the east and west by the said grantee,
north by John McIntosh and D. Y. Alexander McKenzie.

****

Houstoun, Sir Patrick
350 acres in St. Andrew Parish

Granted on June 7, 1774   Grant Book I, page 1018

350 acres bounded on the south by the said grantee and partly
by Murdock McLeod and Forbes, on the northeast by vacant land
and on the west by Donald McLeod.

****

Houstoun, Sir Patrick
150 acres in St. Andrew Parish

Granted on July 5, 1774   Grant Book M, page 47

150 acres bounded on the west by Peter Nephew, west by Sir Patrick Houstoun and ____McCulloch and on the east by the said Patrick Houstoun and Donald McLeod.

****

Houstoun, Sir Patrick
400 acres in St. Andrew Parish

Granted on September 6, 1774   Grant Book M, page 321

400 acres bounded on the west by Sir Patrick Houstoun, north by Sir Patrick Houstoun and Thomas King and southwest by John Bowman.

****

Houstoun, Priscilla
50 acres in St. Andrew Parish

Granted on August 2, 1774   Grant Book H, page 115

50 acres bounded on all sides by land of Sir Patrick Houstoun.

****

Hume, John
1000 acres in St. Andrew Parish

Granted on July 5, 1774   Grant Book M, page 52

1000 acres bounded on the north by the North Branch of the Altamaha River, south by the Three Mile Cut Off Creek and Lachlan McIntosh and west by the Middle Branch of the Altamaha River and vacant marsh.

****

Innis, Susannah, wife of James Innis
50 acres in St. Andrew Parish

Granted on January 3, 1775   Grant Book M, page 890

50 acres bounded on the northwest by William McIntosh, which was originally granted to John Gray, and on the northeast by Jennet McKay.

****

Irwin, Benjamin
200 acres in St. Andrew Parish

Granted on February 5, 1760   Grant Book B, page 353

200 acres bounded on the west by Lewis Creek and on all
other sides by vacant land.

****

Jagger, John
400 acres in St. Andrew Parish

Granted on October 4, 1757   Grant Book A, page 639

400 acres bounded on the southwest by David Miller and on
all other sides by the Sapelo and marshes and creeks of
the same.

****

Jamieson, John
300 acres in St. Andrew Parish

Surveyed on July 18, 1771   Plat Book C, page 106
Granted on November 5, 1771   Grant Book I, page 457

300 acres bounded on the west by the Altamaha River, north
by James Mackay, east by John Jones and south by James
Cantey.

****

Johnson, Lewis and Alexander Wylly
150 acres in St. Andrew Parish

Surveyed on March 11, 1761   Plat Book C, page 320
Granted on January 19, 1773   Grant Book I, page 860

150 acres bounded on the southwest by the Altamaha River and
originally surveyed for Samuel Sanders and thence ordered to
Lewis Johnson and Alexander Wylly on June 2, 1772.

****

Johnson, William
100 acres in St. Andrew Parish

Granted on December 3, 1760   Grant Book C, page 31

100 acres bounded on the south by William Clarke, west by Daniel McKenzie and north and east by a creek and salt marsh.

****

Johnson, William
150 acres in St. Andrew Parish

Surveyed on June 16, 1761   Plat Book C, page 103
Granted on May 21, 1762   Grant Book D, page 126

150 acres bounded on the west by the Altamaha River and on all other sides by vacant land. Surveyed as William Johnston.

****

Johnston, John
450 acres in St. Andrew Parish

Surveyed on October 24, 1771   Plat Book C, page 107
Granted on January 7, 1772   Grant Book I, page 496

450 acres bounded on the east by Clement Martin.

****

Jones, Inigo
450 acres in St. Andrew Parish

Surveyed on June 21, 1771   Plat Book C, page 106
Granted on June 2, 1772   Grant Book I, page 626

450 acres bounded on the southwest by the Altamaha River and on the northwest by Lachlan McGillivray.

****

Jones, James
150 acres in St. Andrew Parish

Granted on January 3, 1775   Grant Book M, page 887

150 acres bounded on the southwest by Lachlan McIntosh, north by vacant land, northeast by William McIntosh and on the northwest by Lachlan McIntosh.

****

Jones, John
500 acres in St. Andrew Parish

Surveyed on August 16, 1760   Plat Book C, page 105
Granted on February 3, 1762   Grant Book D, page 25

500 acres bounded on the south by the Altamaha River and
on the east by the said John Jones.

****

Jones, John
500 acres in St. Andrew Parish

Surveyed on August 16, 1760   Plat Book C, page 105
Granted on February 3, 1762   Grant Book D, page 26

500 acres bounded on the south by the Altamaha River, east
by Thomas King and west by the said John Jones.

****

Jones, John
200 acres in St. Andrew Parish

Granted on August 4, 1767   Grant Book F, page 316

200 acres bounded on the north by William Thomas Harris,
east by marshes of Sapelo River, west by marshes of South
Newport River, and on every other side by land vacant at
the time of the survey, which said tract was heretofore
ordered to Joseph Perry.

****

Jones, Noble
500 acres in St. Andrew Parish

Surveyed on January 31, 1772   Plat Book C, page 106
Granted on May 5, 1772   Grant Book I, page 595

500 acres bounded on the southeast by John Johnson and on
all other sides by vacant land.

****

Jones, Samuel
400 acres in St. Andrew Parish

Surveyed on July 25, 1768   Plat Book C, page 104
Granted on November 1, 1768   Grant Book G, page 212

400 acres bounded on the south by James Andrew and on the
northwest by Lydia Saunders.

                              ****

Jones, Samuel
50 acres in St. Andrew Parish

Surveyed on March 11, 1767   Plat Book C, page 103

50 acres bounded on all sides by vacant land.

                              ****

Jones, William
250 acres in St. Andrew Parish

Surveyed on November 22, 1766   Plat Book C, page 105
Granted on April 7, 1767   Grant Book F, page 189

250 acres bounded on the north by Thomas Carter, south by
Audley Maxwell and Joseph Powell and southwest by William
Baker.

                              ****

Jones, William
600 acres in St. Andrew Parish

Surveyed on August 1, 1769   Plat Book C, page 104
Granted on November 7, 1769   Grant Book G, page 461

600 acres bounded on all sides by vacant land.

                              ****

Jones, William
150 acres in St. Andrew Parish

Surveyed on October 22, 1767   Plat Book C, page 104
Granted on March 6, 1770   Grant Book G, page 552

150 acres bounded on the north by the said William Jones.

Jones, William
50 acres in St. Andrew Parish

Surveyed on May 3, 1773   Plat Book C, page 106
Granted on August 2, 1774   Grant Book H, page 114

50 acres bounded on the south by Goldwire and on all other sides by vacant land.

****

Jones, William
300 acres in St. Andrew Parish

Surveyed on April 25, 1768   Plat Book C, page 104

300 acres bounded on the southeast by the Sapelo River and on the southwest by John Paulson.

****

Kelly, Thomas
200 acres in St. Andrew Parish

Surveyed on May 4, 1760   Plat Book C, pages 118 & 120
Granted on November 3, 1761   Grant Book C, page 277

200 acres bounded on all sides by vacant land.

****

Kelly, Thomas
300 acres in St. Andrew Parish

Surveyed on December 11, 1766   Plat Book C, page 120

300 acres bounded on all sides by vacant land.

****

Kelsall, Roger
400 acres in St. Andrew Parish

Surveyed on June 4, 1772   Plat Book C, page 120
Granted on April 6, 1773   Grant Book I, page 952

400 acres bounded on the south by Sarah Spencer and the said grantee and east by Moses Way. Plat shows public road leading to the Altamaha bounding on the east.

Kelsall, Roger
146 acres in St. Andrew Parish

Granted on September 6, 1774   Grant Book M, page 338

146 acres bounded on the northeast by Moses Way and Richard
Spencer, southwest by Grey Elliott, northwest by William
Davis and southeast by Thomas Smith.

****

Kelsall, Roger and Simon Munro
200 acres in St. Andrew Parish

Granted on February 2, 1768   Grant Book G, page 25

200 acres bounded on the northwest by John Lawson, southeast
by Samuel Sanders and southwest by the Altamaha River. The
tract was originally ordered to John Perkins.

****

Kelsall, Roger and Simons Munroe
300 acres in St. Andrew Parish

Surveyed on February 26, 1762   Plat Book C, page 118

300 acres bounded on the southwest by the Altamaha River,
northwest by William McKormack and vacant land and southeast
by Robert Miller.

****

Kennedy, Donald
150 acres in St. Andrew Parish

Granted on September 30, 1757   Grant Book A, page 475

150 acres bounded on the northeast by George McDonald and
situate at the head of a creek on the Sapelo River.

****

Kid, George
50 acres in St. Andrew Parish

Surveyed on December 20, 1761   Plat Book C, page 118

50 acres bounded on the south by Samuel Fulton, west by Samuel Fulton, north by John Grant and east by Hugh Ross.

****

King, Thomas
200 acres in St. Andrew Parish

Surveyed on May 27, 1762   Plat Book C, page 119
Granted on September 3, 1765   Grant Book E, page 233

200 acres bounded on the north by John MacCulloch and vacant land, east by land of the late Sir Patrick Houstoun, south by Donald Clarke and west by John Grant.

****

King, Thomas
150 acres in St. Andrew Parish

Surveyed on August 27, 1763   Plat Book C, page 119
Granted on September 3, 1765   Grant Book E, page 235

150 acres bounded on the north by Norman McDonals and vacant land, southeast by Moss Grinag and vacant land and southwest by Alexander McKensy.

****

King, Thomas
250 acres in St. Andrew Parish

Surveyed on Febraury 14, 1767   Plat Book C, page 119
Granted on May 5, 1767   Grant Book F, page 236

250 acres bounded on the southeast by John Munro and on the west by Mary McCullock.

****

King, Thomas
150 acres in St. Andrew Parish

Granted on November 1, 1774   Grant Book M, page 679

150 acres bounded on the north by Sir Patrick Houstoun and on all other sides by vacant land.

****

King, Thomas
150 acres in St. Andrew Parish

Surveyed on February 28, 1769   Plat Book C, page 119

150 acres bounded on the northwest by the said Thomas King
and on all other sides by vacant land.

****

Law, Joseph
300 acres in St. Andrew Parish

Surveyed on July 31, 1771   Plat Book C, page 162
Granted on November 5, 1771   Grant Book I, page 459

300 acres bounded on the northeast partly by William Bacon,
on the northwest partly by James Stewart and on all other
sides by vacant land.

****

Law, Joseph
250 acres in St. Andrew Parish

Surveyed on August 22, 1771   Plat Book C, page 161
Granted on March 3, 1772   Grant Book I, page 532

250 acres bounded on all sides by vacant land.

****

Lawson, John
500 acres in St. Andrew Parish

Surveyed on September 1, 1761   Plat Book C, page 158
Granted on May 21, 1762   Grant Book D, page 102

500 acres bounded on the southwest by the Altamaha River and
on the northwest by Captain John Gray.

****

LeConte, John Eaton and William LeConte
400 acres in St. Andrew Parish

Granted on August 2, 1774   Grant Book M, page 215

400 acres bounded on the southeast by William Davis and Thomas Smith, southwest by John McLuer and Thomas Cox and northeast by Grey Elliott and Thomas Sullivant.

****

LeConte, John Eaton and William LeConte
360 acres in St. Andrew Parish

Surveyed on February 27, 1772   Plat Book C, page 162

360 acres bounded on the north by Charles West and Stephen Williams, east by Charles West, south by Grey Elliott and west by Thomas Sullivant.

****

LeConte, John Eatton and William LeConte
25 acres in St. Andrew Parish

Surveyed on February 25, 1772   Plat Book C, page 162
Granted on September 1, 1772   Grant Book H, page 88

25 acres bounded on the southwest by Francis Lee, southeast by Elisha Butler and northeast by William Elliott.

****

LeConte, John Eatton and William LeConte
100 acres in St. Andrew Parish

Surveyed on June 10, 1772   Plat Book C, page 161
Granted on October 6, 1772   Grant Book I, page 763

100 acres bounded on the northwest by William Davis, west by William Simpson and Moses Way, southeast by Richard Spencer and northeast by Thomas Smith.

****

LeConte, William
500 acres in St. Andrew and St. John Parishes

Surveyed on August 31, 1770   Plat Book C, page 161
Granted on December 4, 1770   Grant Book I, page 221

500 acres bounded on all sides by vacant land.

****

Lee, Francis
200 acres in St. Andrew Parish

Granted on December 4, 1759   Grant Book B, page 323

200 acres bounded on the south by James McKay and on the southeast by Butler.

****

Lester, Campbell
100 acres in St. Andrew Parish

Granted on September 6, 1774   Grant Book M, page 344

100 acres bounded on the southeast by Alexander McDonald and vacant land and southwest by John Gray and Angus McIntosh.

****

Lewis, Abraham
100 acres in St. Andrew Parish

Surveyed on July 4, 1761   Plat Book C, page 160
Granted on December 1, 1767   Grant Book F, page 425

100 acres bounded on the north by Lewis' Creek, west by John Lewis, south by Cut Off Creek and east by Isaac Lewis.

****

Lewis, Benjamin
100 acres in St. Andrew Parish

Surveyed on February 9, 1762   Plat Book C, page 160
Granted on May 21, 1762   Grant Book D, page 137

100 acres bounded on the west by John Lewis, south by Lewis' Creek and east by James McClelland.

****

Lewis, Isaac
100 acres in St. Andrew Parish

Surveyed on October 6, 1760   Plat Book C, page 160
Granted on March 3, 1767   Grant Book F, page 123

100 acres bounded on the south by the Altamaha River and north by Lewis' Creek.

****

Lewis, Jacob
150 acres in St. Andrew Parish

Surveyed on May 30, 1770   Plat Book C, page 161
Granted on June 5, 1771   Grant Book I, page 353

150 acres surveyed for Jacob Lewis and then ordered to John Simpson on April 2, 1771. Granted to John Simpson.

****

Lewis, John
50 acres in St. Andrew Parish

Surveyed June 16, 1761   Plat Book C, page 160
Granted on February 3, 1762   Grant Book D, page 50

50 acres bounded on the east by Samuel Lewis and on the south by Lewis Creek.

****

Lewis, John
100 acres in St. Andrew Parish

Surveyed on August 1, 1760   Plat Book C, page 159

100 acres bounded on the north by Lewis Creek and on the south and west by Samuel Lewis.

****

Lewis, Joseph
100 acres in St. Andrew Parish

Surveyed on August 14, 1765   Plat Book C, page 160
Granted on March 3, 1767   Grant Book F, page 125

100 acres bounded on the south by William Johnson and on all other sides by vacant land.

****

Lewis, Samuel
400 acres in St. Andrew Parish

Surveyed on August 5, 1759   Plat Book C, page 159
Granted on September 25, 1760   Grant Book B, page 532

400 acres bounded on the north by Lewis' Creek and south by
the Altamaha River. The plat of survey also shows that this
is bounded by Rutherfords Creek and Cut Off Creek.

****

Lewis, Smauel
100 acres in St. Andrew Parish

Surveyed on February 26, 1760   Plat Book C, page 158
Granted on September 25, 1760   Grant Book C, page 403

100 acres bounded on all sides by vacant land.

****

Lewis Samuel
50 acres in St. Andrew Parish

Surveyed on May 12, 1760   Plat Book C, page 159
Granted on January 5, 1762   Grant Book D, page 11

50 acres bounded, according to the plat of survey, on the
southwest by Lewis Creek and on the southeast by Marmaduke
Perry.

****

Lewis, Samuel
100 acres in St. Andrew Parish

Granted on March 3, 1767   Grant Book F, page 121

100 acres bounded on the northeast by Lewis' Creek and on the
west and south by Samuel Lewis.

****

Lewis, Samuel
50 acres in St. Andrew Parisg

Surveyed on June 16, 1761   Plat Book C, page 159

50 acres bounded on the south by Lewis Creek, east by Samuel Fulton and west by John Lewis. The plat of survey states that this is a resurvey.

****

Lightonston, John
200 acres in St. Andrew Parish

Surveyed on April 14, 1757   Plat Book C, page 362
Granted on March 3, 1767   Grant Book F, page 127

200 acres bounded on the southwest by Little Sapelo River, Originally surveyed for John Todd, thence ordered John Laghteston on September 2, 1766.

****

Lines, Isaac
300 acres in St. Andrew Parish

Granted on July 1, 1760   Grant Book B, page 394

300 acres bounded on the east by John Grant and on all other sides by vacant land.

****

Long, William
300 acres in St. Andrew Parish

Surveyed on February 8, 1770   Plat Book C, page 158

300 acres bounded on the southwest by Alexander McDonald and on all other sides by vacant land.

****

Lucena, James
1000 acres in St. Andrew Parish

Surveyed on August 22, 1770   Plat Book C, page 162
Granted on January 7, 1772   Grant Book I, page 498

1000 acres bounded on the south by James Maxwell and Joseph Butler and all other sides by vacant land.

****

MacBean, John
100 acres in St. Andrew Parish

Granted on April 5, 1757   Grant Book A, page 362

100 acres in the district of Darien bounded on all sides
by vacant land.

****

Mackay, Angus
50 acres in St. Andrew Parish

Surveyed on November 18, 1759   Plat Book C, page 408

50 acres bounded on all sides by vacant land.

****

Mackay, Daniel, Sr.
150 acres in St. Andrew Parish

Surveyed on February 20, 1756   Plat Book C, page 228
Granted on February 7, 1758   Grant Book A, page 564

150 acres in the district of Darien bounded on all sides by
vacant land.

****

Mackay, James
50 acres in St. Andrew Parish

Surveyed on May 14, 1760   Plat Book C, page 253 & 407
Granted on October 29, 1765   Grant Book E, page 264

50 acres bounded on all sides by vacant land.

****

Mackay, James
200 acres in St. Andrew Parish

Granted on June 6, 1769   Grant Book G, page 335

200 acres bounded on the west by the said James Mackay.

****

Mackay, John
50 acres in St. Andrew Parish

Surveyed on June 29, 1759   Plat Book C, page 257
Granted on April 13, 1761   Grant Book C, page 156

50 acres bounded on the northwest by Sapelo River and surveyed as John McKay.

****

Mackay, Roderick
500 acres in St. Andrew Parish

Surveyed on July 21, 1766   Plat Book C, page 259
Granted on March 3, 1767   Grant Book F, page 134

500 acres bounded on the southeast by land formerly surveyed for John McIntosh, northwest by land granted Hugh Clark and northeast by the Sapelo River.

****

Mackay, Roderick
450 acres in St. Andrew Parish

Surveyed on July 25, 1772   Plat Book C, page 297

450 acres bounded on the east by Daniel McKinzey and north west by Robert Baillie.

****

Mackey, William
50 acres in St. Andrew Parish

Surveyed on September 22, 1772   Plat Book C, page 280

50 acres bounded on the northeast and east by the south branch of Sapelo River, south by Roderick McKay and west by Robert Baillie.

****

Mackintosh. George
500 acres in St. Andrew Parish

Granted on February 11, 1757   Grant Book A, page 313

500 acres situate in the district of Darien and bounded on
all sides by vacant land.

****

Mackintosh, John
150 acres in St. Andrew Parish

Granted on February 11, 1757   Grant Book A, page 309

150 acres situate in the district of Darien and bounded on
all sides by the Altamaha River and the marshes.

****

Mackintosh, John
434 acres in St. Andrew Parish

Granted on February 11, 1757   Grant Book A, page 312

434 acres situate in the district of Sapelo and bounded on
the northeast by the marshes of Newport River.

****

Mackintosh, John
350 acres in St. Andrew Parish

Granted on April 5, 1757   Grant Book A, page 361

350 acres situate in the district of Sapelo and bounded on
the northwest by William Mackintosh.

****

Mackintosh, William
400 acres in St. Andrew Parish

Granted on March 7, 1769   Grant Book G, page 280

400 acres bounded on the east by John McKintosh, northwest
by Roderick McKay and east by John McBane.

****

Maddock, Mordecai
400 acres on St. Andrew Parish

Granted on November 1, 1774   Grant Book M, page 688

400 acres bounded on the northeast by Robert Baillie and on all other sides by vacant land.

****

Mahanahan, Charles
100 acres in St. Andrew Parish

Surveyed on January 27, 1771   Plat Book C, page 275
Granted on October 1, 1771   Grant Book I, page 437

100 acres originally surveyed for Mahanahan, then ordered to John Oates on July 2, 1771. Granted to John Oates.

****

Marrett, Joseph
100 acres in St. Andrew Parish

Surveyed on February 15, 1772   Plat Book C, page 278
Granted on August 2, 1774   Grant Book M, page 232

The plat of survey shows that this tract is bounded on the east by Joseph Marret and on all other sides vacant.

****

Martin, Clement
800 acres in St. Andrew Parish

Surveyed on June 23, 1769   Plat Book C, page 258
Granted on October 3, 1769   Grant Book G, page 438

800 acres bounded on all sides by vacant land.

****

Martin, Clement, Jr.
1000 acres in St. Andrew Parish

Granted on May 1, 1770   Grant Book I, page 7

100 acres bounded on the southwest by land of Clement Martin.

****

Martin, Clement, Sr.
100 acres in St. Andrew Parish

Granted on November 1, 1774   Grant Book M, page 709

100 acres bounded on the north by Thomas Camber, east by the salt marshes of Doboy River and south by Lachlan McIntosh.

****

Martin, John
250 acres in St. Andrew Parish

Surveyed on September 18, 1761   Plat Book C, page 235 & 408
Granted on January 4, 1763   Grant Book D, page 274

250 acres bounded on the east by Moses Way and on all other sides by vacant land.

****

Martin, John
250 acres in St. Andrew Parish

Surveyed July 13, 1762   Plat Book C, page 226
Granted on September 2, 1766   Grant Book E, page 364

250 acres bounded on the north by Daniel Donnam and on the northwest by James Mackay.

****

Martin, John
150 acres in St. Andrew Parish

Surveyed on November 10, 1772   Plat Book C, page 208
Granted on May 4, 1773   Grant Book I, page 987

150 acres bounded on the northwest by land run for Hugh Ross and on the south by Donald McIntosh.

****

Mattier, Lewis
250 acres in St. Andrew Parish

Surveyed on May 1, 1773   Plat Book C, page 292
Granted on July 5, 1774   Grant Book M, page 66

250 acres bounded by land of the said Lewis Mattier on the northwest and on the northeast by William Mills.

****

Maxwell, James
500 acres in St. Andrew Parish

Surveyed on June 21, 1769   Plat Book C, page 210
Granted on January 19, 1773   Grant Book I, page 870

500 acres bounded on the northwest by James McKay, on the
southwest partly by Joseph Butler and on all other sides by
vacant land.

****

Maybank, Andrew
300 acres in St. Andrew Parish

Surveyed on April 14, 1772   Plat Book C, page 279
Granted on July 7, 1772   Grant Book I, page 683

300 acres bounded on the south by John Bohun Girardeau and on
all other sides by vacant land.

****

Maybank, Andrew
300 acres in St. Andrew Parish

Surveyed on February 11, 1772   Plat Book C, page 279
Granted on July 7, 1772   Grant Book I, page 692

300 acres bounded on the west by _____Mattier and ___Miller,
east by _____Cocks, south by the said grantee and north by
vacant land.

****

McBean, John
100 acres in St. Andrew Parish

Granted on May 1, 1759   Grant Book B, page 172

100 acres in the district of Darien, bounded on all sides by
vacant land.

****

McBean, John
100 acres in St. Andrew Parish

Surveyed on June 27, 1757   Plat Book C, page 437

100 acres situate in the district of Sapelo and bounded on all sides by vacant land.

＊＊＊＊

McCartin, Clement
1000 acres in St. Andrew Parish

Surveyed on January 17, 1770   Plat Book C, page 245

1000 acres bounded on the southeast by Clement Martin and on all other sides by vacant land.

＊＊＊＊

McCarty, Florence
250 acres in St. Andrew Parish

Surveyed on August 22, 1763   Plat Book C, page 238
Granted on April 3, 1764   Grant Book D, page 406

250 acres bounded on the northeast by the said Florence McCarty and Hugh Ross and west by Benjamin Farley.

＊＊＊＊

McCleland, Brice
150 acres in St. Andrew Parish

Surveyed on July 24, 1769   Plat Book C, page 233
Granted on December 5, 1769   Grant Book G, page 477

150 acres bounded on all sides by vacant land.

＊＊＊＊

McCleland, James
500 acres in St. Andrew Parish

Surveyed on February 29, 1760   Plat Book C, page 257 & 407

500 acres bounded on the east by Isaac Lyons and David Fulton, south by James McCleland and west by Samuel Fulton.

＊＊＊＊

McCleland, John
118 acres in St. Andrew Parish

Surveyed on Fenruary 8, 1764   Plat Book C, page 220
Granted on March 6, 1764   Grant Book D, page 391

118 acres bounded on the west by David Fulton, north by
Samuel Fulton, east by John McCullough and south by the
said John McCleland.

****

McCleland, John
86 acres in St. Andrew Parish

Surveyed on February 9, 1764   Plat Book C, page 226
Granted on March 6, 1764   Grant Book D, page 392

86 acres bounded on the north by Benjamin Erwin and the said
John McCleland, east and south by the said John McCleland
and on the southwest by Lewis' Creek.

****

McCleland, John
160 acres in St. Andrew Parish

Granted on January 19, 1773   Grant Book I, page 873

160 acres bounded on the north and west by the said grantee,
east by James McCleland and south by Lewis' Creek.

****

McCleland, John
443 acres in St. Andrew Parish

Surveyed on December 28, 1771   Plat Book C, page 293

443 acres bounded on the west by John McCleland, Benjamin
Ervins and David Witherspoon, north by John McCleland and
Mary McCleland, east by James McCleland and south by Lewis'
Creek. This surveyed in 2 tracts, 161 acres and 282 acres.

****

McCleland, John
400 acres in St. Andrew Parish

Surveyed on February 25, 1760   Plat Book C, page 217 & 405

400 acres bounded on the east by James McCleland, north by James McCleland and Samuel Fulton, west by Irwin and south by Lewis' Creek.

****

McCleland, John
118 acres in St. Andrew Parish

Surveyed on November 12, 1761   Plat Book C, page 222

118 acres bounded on the west by David Witherspoon.

****

McCleland, Mary
300 acres in St. Andrew Parish

Surveyed on May 17, 1769   Plat Book C, page 256
Granted on October 2, 1770   Grant Book I, page 174

300 acres bounded on the south by James McCleland and on all other sides by vacant land.

****

McClelland, James
350 acres in St. Andrew Parish

Surveyed on August 12, 1760   Plat Book C, page 258 & 405
Granted on May 21, 1762   Grant Book D, page 83

350 acres bounded on the east by David Fulton, north by Mary McClelland, widow, west by John McClelland and on the south and southeast by Lewis' Creek.

****

McClelland, Mary
500 acres in St. Andrew Parish

Granted on May 21, 1762   Grant Book D, page 82

500 acres bounded on the west by Samuel Fulton, south by James McClelland, east by David Fulton and Isaac Lines.

****

McCleod, Donald
150 acres in St. Andrew Parish

Surveyed on January 7, 1769   Plat Book C, page 254
Granted on July 4, 1769   Grant Book G, page 366

150 acres bounded on the northeast by the said Donald McCleod,
southeast by Murdock McCleod and surveyed as Donald McCloud.

****

McCloud, Murdock
50 acres in St. Andrew Parish

Surveyed on February 17, 1767   Plat Book C, page 258
Granted on May 5, 1767   Grant Book F, page 246

50 acres bounded on the south by the said Murdock McCloud
and on all other sides by vacant land.

****

McCloud, Murdock
100 acres in St. Andrew Parish

Surveyed on February 19, 1756   Plat Book C, page 249

100 acres bounded on the north by McCloud and on all other
sides by vacant land.

****

McCluer, John
100 acres in St. Andrew Parish

Surveyed on October 21, 1772   Plat Book C, page 291

100 acres bounded on the southeast by John McCluer, southwest
by Thomas Cox, northeast by John and William LeConte.

****

McCormack, William
100 acres in St. Andrew Parish

Surveyed on February 27, 1762   Plat Book C, page 250
Granted on June 5, 1764   Grant Book E, page 16

100 acres bounded on the west by the Altamaha River and on the southeast by Durham Hancock.

****

McCorrie, Andrew
400 acres in St. Andrew Parish

Surveyed on October 29, 1768   Plat Book C, page 218
Granted on March 7, 1769   Grant Book G, page 281

400 acres bounded on the southwest and southeast by Abraham Bird and on the west by William Jones, and surveyed as Andrew McCorried.

****

McCulloch, John
426 acres in St. Andrew Parish

Surveyed June 30, 1761   Plat Book C, page 249 & 405
Granted on November 2, 1762   Grant Book D, page 224

426 acres bounded on the south by the Altamaha River and Lewis Creek, west by Samuel Fulton, north by the said John McCulloch and east by Lieutenant Robert Baillie.

****

McCulloch, John
500 acres in St. Andrew Parish

Surveyed on February 27, 1760   Plat Book C, page 212 & 407
Granted on November 2, 1762   Grant Book D, page 225

500 acres bounded on the north by Donald Clark and Cat Head Creek and on the west by Samuel Fulton.

****

McCulloch, John
100 acres in St. Andrew Parish

Surveyed on May 27, 1762   Plat Book C, page 247
Granted on September 1, 1767   Grant Book F, page 410

100 acres bounded on the west by John Grant and all other sides by vacant land.

McCulloch, John
100 acres in St. Andrew Parish

Surveyed on May 18, 1769   Plat Book C, page 263
Granted on August 1, 1769   Grant Book G, page 393

100 acres bounded on all sides by vacant land.

****

McCullock, John
50 acres in St. Andrew Parish

Surveyed on November 11, 1771   Plat Book C, page 278
Granted on May 5, 1772   Grant Book H, page 81

50 acres bounded on the west by land of the said grantee
and south and east by Sir Patrick Houstoun.

****

McCullough, Mary, widow of Nathaniel, in trust for children
500 acres in St. Andrew Parish

Granted on August 2, 1763   Grant Book D, page 318

500 acres bounded on the northeast by Cat Head Creek and
southeast by Lachlan McIntosh. See Plat Book C, page 260.

****

McCullough, Mary, widow
150 acres in St. Andrew Parish

Surveyed on February 14, 1767   Plat Book C, page 218
Granted on December 6, 1768   Grant Book G, page 236

150 acres bounded on the south and west by John Perkins, east
by Thomas King and southeast by John Munro. The plat of
survey states, "In trust for her six children, Tannet, Elizabeth,
William, Nathaniel James, John and Martha, the children of
Nathaniel McCullough, deceased.

****

McCulloch, Nathaniel
100 acres in St. Andrew Parish

Granted on November 1, 1774   Grant Book M, page 710

100 acres bounded on the east by Lewis Creek and on all other sides by vacant land.

****

McCulloch, Nathaniel
100 acres in St. Andrew Parish

Surveyed on October 3, 1770   Plat Book C, page 275

100 acres bounded on the southeast by George Gray and on all other sides by vacant land.

****

McCulloch, Nathaniel
500 acres in St. Andrew Parish

Surveyed on November 25, 1760   Plat Book C, page 260

500 acres bounded on the northeast by Cat Head Creek and on the southeast by Lachlan McIntosh.

****

McCulloch, Nathaniel
500 acres in St. Andrew Parish

Surveyed on May 28, 1761   Plat Book C, page 260

500 acres bounded on the northeast by Cat Head Creek and on the southeast by Lachlan McIntosh. See grant to Mary McCulloch on page 318, Grant Book D, as widow of Nathaniel. This is the same tract.

****

McCulloch, William
345 acres in St. Andrew Parish

Surveyed on November 26, 1760   Plat Book C, page 235

345 acres bounded on the south by Donald Clark, west by John Grant and McDonald's 50 acre tract (see original detached plat). The original plat shows this tract bounded on the east by Sir Patrick Houstoun. The original warrant says the land was located on the Altamaha River between Cathead Creek and the Ohoopie River.

McCullum, James
150 acres in St. Andrew Parish

Surveyed on February 21, 1757   Plat Book C, page 406

150 acres bounded on all sides by vacant land.

****

McDonald, Alexander
150 acres in St. Andrew Parish

Granted on July 4, 1758   Grant Book B, page 47

150 acres in the district of Sapelo bounded on all sides by vacant land.

****

McDonald, Alexander
50 acres in St. Andrew Parish

Surveyed on February 16, 1756   Plat Book C, page 216
Granted on November 7, 1758   Grant Book B, page 425

50 acres bounded on the southeast by the said McDonald and on all other sides by vacant land.

****

McDonald, Alexander
150 acres in St. Andrew Parish

Surveyed on October 24, 1761   Plat Book C, page 225
Granted on November 1, 1774   Grant Book M, page 707

150 acres bounded on all sides by vacant land.

****

McDonald, Alexander
50 acres in St. Andrew Parish

Surveyed on January 21, 1769   Plat Book C, page 234
Granted on June 7, 1774   Grant Book H, page 127

Originally surveyed for Alexander McDonald but ordered to William McIntosh on March 5, 1771. Bounded on the south by Alexander McDonald. Granted to William McIntosh.

McDonald, Archibald
150 acres in St. Andrew Parish

Granted on December 6, 1763   Grant Book D, page 359

150 acres bounded on all sides by vacnat land.

****

McDonald, Archibald
250 acres in St. Andrew Parish

Surveyed on January 28, 1771   Plat Book C, page 273
Granted on May 5, 1772   Grant Book I, page 598

250 acres bounded on the southwest by the said grantee and
on the southeast by William McDonald.

****

McDonald, Charles
100 acres in St. Andrew Parish

Surveyed - no date   Plat Book C, page 254
Granted on September 1, 1767   Grant Book F, page 360

100 acres bounded on the southeast by James Munroe and William
McKay and on every other side by land vacant, which said tract
includes 50 acres of land heretofore ordered to and surveyed
for Norm & McDonald and 50 acres heretofore ordered and surveyed
for Donald Ross.

****

McDonald, Charles
150 acres in St. Andrew Parish

Surveyed on March 26, 1771   Plat Book C, page 273
Granted on August 6, 1771   Grant Book I, page 387

150 acres bounded on the southeast by John McDonald and on
the southwest by James Clark.

****

McDonald, Donald
200 acres in St. Andrew Parish

Granted on April 5, 1757   Grant Book A, page 433

200 acres at the head of the south branch of the South Newport River and bounded on all sides by vacant land.

****

McDonald, Donald
100 acres in St. Andrew Parish

Surveyed on July 13, 1759   Plat Book C, page 226 & 405
Granted on February 7, 1764   Grant Book D, page 382

100 acres bounded on the north by the head of Newport River, west and north by Hearts land, west by Farley and southeast by the said Donald McDonald.

****

McDonald, Donald
100 acres in St. Andrew Parish

Surveyed on June 2, 1764   Plat Book C, page 248
Granted on March 5, 1765   Grant Book E, page 124

100 acres bounded on the northwest by Donald McKay.

****

McDonald, Donald
300 acres in St. Andrew Parish

Granted on June 7, 1774   Grant Book I, page 1034

300 acres bounded on the southeast by the Sapelo River, west by John Doulson and on all other sides by land vacnat at the time of the survey, the same having been heretofore ordered and surveyed for William Jones.

****

McDonald, Donald
160 acres in St. Andrew Parish

Surveyed on January 2, 1771   Plat Book C, page 279
Granted on August 2, 1774   Grant Book M, page 233

160 acres bounded on the south by ___Southerland, west by ___ Gwinnett and east by Polson. Surveyed as 150 acres.

****

McDonald, George
150 acres in St. Andrew Parish

Surveyed on November 20, 1755   Plat Book C, page 251
Granted on October 2, 1759   Grant Book B, page 207

150 acres in the district of Sapelo and bounded on the
northwest by Donald Kennedy.

                          ****

McDonald, George
150 acres in St. Andrew Parish

Granted on October 29, 1765   Grant Book E, page 261

150 acres bounded on the south by Donald Ross and on all
other sides by vacant land.

                          ****

McDonald, George
50 acres in St. Andrew Parish

Surveyed on November 23, 1770   Plat Book C, page 273
Granted on January 7, 1772   Grant Book H, page 67

50 acres bounded on the south and east by John McBean,
on the north and northwest partly by John McDonald, on
our bounty pursuant to our Royal Proclamation.

                          ****

McDonald, John
100 acres in St. Andrew Parish

Granted on February 7, 1758   Grant Book A, page 562

100 acres in the district of Darien known as Fort Swamp.

                          ****

McDonald, John
200 acres in St. Andrew Parish

Surveyed on January 17, 1769   Plat Book M, page 56
Granted on July 4, 1769   Grant Book G, page 365

200 acres bounded on the southeast by Norman McDonald.

McDonald, John
150 acres in St. Andrew Parish

Surveyed on May 29, 1769   Plat Book C, page 216
Granted on May 1, 1770   Grant Book I, page 8

150 acres bounded on the west partly by land of John McBains
and on all other sides by vacant land.

****

McDonald, John
114 acres in St. Andrew Parish

Granted on July 5, 1774   Grant Book M, page 77

114 acres bounded on the southwest by John McDonald, George
McDonald and John McBean, southeast by William McIntosh,
northeast by Roderick McKay and northwest by Hugh Clark.

****

McDonald, John
286 acres in St. Andrew Parish

Granted on November 1774   Grant Book M, page 689

286 acres bounded on the north and south by George McIntosh,
southeast by High Morrison, Simon Fraiser and Ann McIntosh.

****

McDonald, John
50 acres in Sr. Andrew Parish

Surveyed on May 24, 1760   Plat Book C, page 227 & 406

50 acres bounded on the northwest by Daniel Ross and on all
other sides by vacant land.

****

McDonald, Norman
100 acres in St. Andrew Parish

Granted on February 7, 1758   Grant Book B, page 449

100 acres in the district of Darien bounded on all sides by
vacnat land.

McDonald, Norman
100 acres in St. Andrew Parish

Surveyed on October 27, 1759   Plat Book C, page 233
Surveyed on November 4, 1760   Plat Book C, page 407

100 acres bounded on the northeast by Norman McDonald and on all other sides by vacant land.

****

McDonald, William
300 acres in St. Andrew Parish

Surveyed on August 17, 1769   Plat Book C, page 213
Granted on March 6, 1770   Grant Book G, page 556

300 acres bounded on the southeast by George McDonald and on all other sides by vacant land.

****

McGillivray, Lachlan
392 acres in St. Andrew Parish

Surveyed on January 22, 1761   Plat Book C, page 221
Granted on March 6, 1764   Grant Book D, page 388

392 acres bounded on the northeast and southeast by Nathaniel McCullough, Cat Head Creek and Lachlan McIntosh, on the west by Robert Baillie and William McKay.

****

McGillivray, Lachlan
750 acres in St. Andrew Parish

Surveyed on July 29, 1769   Plat Book C, page 228
Granted on October 3, 1769   Grant Book G, page 440

750 acres bounded on the southwest by the Altamaha River. The plat of survey shows the "Florida Path" on the northwest side.

****

McIntosh, Angus
100 acres in St. Andrew Parish

Granted on October 2, 1759   Grant Book B, page 194

100 acres in the district of Sapelo bounded on the northeast
by Alexander McDonald.

****

McIntosh, Angus
100 acres in St. Andrew Parish

Granted on October 2, 1759   Grant Book B, page 195

100 acres in the district of Sapelo and bounded on the
southeast by marsh land.

****

McIntosh, Angus
100 acres in St. Andrew Parish

Surveyed on January 1, 1760   Plat Book C, page 224 & 406
Granted on October 6, 1772   Grant Book I, page 765

100 acres bounded on the northeast by the said grantee and
on all other sides by marshes and vacant land.

****

McIntosh, Anne
450 acres in St. Andrew Parish

Granted on December 4, 1759   Grant Book B, page 344

450 acres in the Fifth Swamp in the district of Darien.

****

McIntosh, Donald
100 acres in St. Andrew Parish

Surveyed on July 12, 1759   Plat Book C, page 249 & 406
Granted on May 21, 1762   Grant Book D, page 138

100 acres bounded on the south by Donalds. The plat of survey
shows this tract was bounded on the south by Donald McIntosh.

****

McIntosh, George
88 acres in St. Andrew Parish

Surveyed on May 17, 1760   Plat Book C, page 264
Granted on April 13, 1761   Grant Book D, page 337

88 acres bounded on the southwest by George McIntosh.

                        ****

McIntosh, George
200 acres in St. Andrew Parish

Surveyed on January 24, 1767   Plat Book C, page 253
Granted on May 5, 1767   Grant Book F, page 249

200 acres bounded on the southwest by land surveyed for Joseph Stevens and Thomas Stephens.

                        ****

McIntosh, George
500 acres in St. Andrew Parish

Surveyed on May 9, 1767   Plat Book C, page 240
Granted on June 2, 1767   Grant Book F, page 276

500 acres bounded on the north by Roderick McLeod, east by John McIntosh, south by the Sapelo River and on the west by land laid out for John Gray.

                        ****

McIntosh, George
300 acres in St. Andrew Parish

Surveyed on December 8, 1770   Plat Book C, page 445
Granted on May 7, 1771   Grant Book I, page 313

300 acres bounded on the northeast partly by land run for Christian Rolland and on all other sides by vacant land.

                        ****

McIntosh, George
200 acres in St. Andrew Parish

Granted on May 7, 1771   Grant Book I, page 314

200 acres bounded on the south by land run out for James Green and by vacant land, on the east partly by vacant land and partly by the said tract run out for James Green, north by vacant land, west by vacant land and partly by land run out for Christian Rolland.

****

McIntosh, George
150 acres in St. Andrew Parish

Granted on April 7, 1772   Grant Book I, page 568

150 acres bounded on the east by the said grantee and on all other sides by vacant land.

****

McIntosh, George
300 acres in St. Andrew Parish

Surveyed on November 10, 1772   Plat Book C, page 292
Granted on June 7, 1774   Grant Book I, page 1051

300 acres bounded on the southeast by Angus McIntosh and George McIntosh.

****

McIntosh, George
1000 acres in St. Andrew Parish

Surveyed on April 8, 1773   Plat Book C, page 290
Granted on June 7, 1774   Grant Book I, page 1052

1000 acres bounded on the northwest and the southwest by vacant land and on all other sides by land run out for the said grantee.

****

McIntosh, George
250 acres in St. Andrew Parish

Granted on August 2, 1774   Grant Book M, page 216

250 acres bounded on the east by George McIntosh and on all other sides by vacant land.

McIntosh, George
500 acres in St. Andrew Parish

Granted on August 2, 1774   Grant Book M, page 217

500 acres bounded on the east and southeast by George McIntosh.

***

****

McIntosh, George
350 acres in St. Andrew Parish

Granted on August 2, 1774   Grant Book M, page 218

350 acres bounded on the west by George McIntosh and McKenzie
and on the north by James Stuart.

****

McIntosh, George
500 acres in St. Andrew Parish

Granted on August 2, 1774   Grant Book M, page 219

500 acres bounded on the south and southeast by the Altamaha
River, west by Herds Island Creek and north by Herds Island,
marshes of said island.

****

McIntosh, George
400 acres in St. Andrew and St. John Parish

Granted on September 6, 1774   Grant Book M, page 350

400 acres bounded on the north by land run our for John
McIntosh and William Elliott, west by land run out for
Joseph Gibbons, south by land run out for Robert Stuart
and William Norton and east by vacant marsh.

****

McIntosh, George
500 acres in St. Andrew Parish

Granted on September 6, 1774   Grant Book M, page 351

500 acres bounded on the northwest by vacant land and on all
other sides by the said George McIntosh.

****

McIntosh, George
100 acres in St. Andrew Parish

Granted on October 4, 1774   Grant Book M, page 576

100 acres bounded on the west by Christian Rolland and on all other sides by George McIntosh.

****

McIntosh, George
350 acres in St. Andrew Parish

Granted on November 1, 1774   Grant Book M, page 692

350 acres bounded on the east by Donald McIntosh, northwest by Hugh Ross, John Martin and Donald McDonald and on the south by George McIntosh.

****

McIntosh, George
200 acres in St. Andrew Parish

Surveyed on December 8, 1770   Plat Book C, page 274

200 acres bounded on the south by Jennit Graham and southwest by Christopher Rolland.

****

McIntosh, George
200 acres in St. Andrew Parish

Surveyed on June 29, 1771   Plat Book C, page 209

200 acres bounded on the east by McKinzie, southwest, west and north by the said George McIntosh and includes 100 acres formerly run out for Mrs. Grame.

****

McIntosh, John
300 acres in St. Andrew Parish

Surveyed on August 28, 1755   Plat Book C, page 237
Granted on May 1, 1759   Grant Book B, page 101

300 acres bounded on all sides by vacant land.

McIntosh, John
500 acres in St. Andrew Parish

Granted on December 3, 1760   Grant Book D, page 64

500 acres bounded on the south and east by Sapelo River and
the marshes thereof and on the west by William Harper.

****

McIntosh, John, son of William
40 acres in St. Andrew Parish

Surveyed on January 23, 1771   Plat Book C, page 272
Granted on June 5, 1771   Grant Book H, page 58

40 acres bounded on the south by Woodlands River and on
the east and west by salt marsh.

****

McIntosh, John (D)
66 acres in St. Andrew Parish

Surveyed on September 2, 1757   Plat Book C, page 249
Granted on April 13, 1761   Grant Book D, page 336

66 acres bounded on all sides by vacant land.

****

McIntosh, Lachlan
500 acres in St. Andrew Parish

Granted on July 4, 1758   Grant Book A, page 653

500 acres, an island in Altamaha River opposite Darien, bounded
on all sides by the said river and branches thereof.

****

McIntosh, Lachlan
100 acres in St. Andrew Parish

Surveyed on April 30, 1765   Plat Book C, page 263
Granted on Ocotber 31, 1765   Grant Book E, page 314

100 acres bounded on the southwest by Cathead Creek and on the
northwest by John Holms.

McIntosh, Lachlan
150 acres in St. Andrew Parish

Surveyed on December 5, 1766   Plat Book C, page 225
Granted on February 3, 1767   Grant Book F, page 73

150 acres being an island in the Altamaha River and bounded
on every side by the said river. The plat of survey states
that this tract is in St. Patricks Parish but it could not
be since the Altamaha River is not part of St. Patrick
Parish. The grant says St. Andrew Parish and maps show that
it is.

****

McIntosh, Lachlan
500 acres in St. Andrew Parish

Surveyed May 18, 1767   Plat Book C, page 223
Granted on October 4, 1768   Grant Book G, page 198

500 acres bounded on the south by Isaac Lyons and on the
east by John Grant and Peter Nephew.

****

McIntosh, Lachlan
1200 acres in St. Andrew Parish

Surveyed on August 3, 1772   Plat Book C, page 293
Granted on October 6, 1772   Grant Book I, page 749

1200 acres on an island opposite to Darien, the same being
surplus measure contained therein, the said island having
formerly been granted to the said grantee and surveyed for
500 acres only, but is now found to contain in the whole
1700 acres, bounded on all sides by the Altamaha River and
the branches thereof. The plat shows this bounded by
Governor Wright's Island, Black Island, John Jamieson's Island
and Henry Lawrence or Britain Island.

****

McIntosh, Lachlan
1000 acres in St. Andrew Parish

Surveyed on April 1, 1771   Plat Book C, page 283
Granted on January 19, 1773   Grant Book I, page 874

1000 acres bounded on the southeast by Thomas King, John Munro and Giles Moore. The plat of survey states that this is bounded on the west by John Bowman and shows Giles Moore and Gilmore.

****

McIntosh, Lachlan
360 acres in St. Andrew Parish

Surveyed on November 5, 1772   Plat Book C, page 297
Granted on June 7, 1774   Grant Book I, page 1031

360 acres in 2 adjoining pieces of surplus land, that is to say, 310 acres, part thereof bounded on the southwest by the Altamaha River, northwest by Mary McCulloch, northeast by land surveyed for John Munro and Cat Head Creek, southeast by the said grantee in a tract originally granted for 500 acres, but which on a resurvey is found to contain the said surplus of 310 acres of land, and 50 acres, the remaining part thereof bounded on the southwest by Cat Head Creek and the surplus of the 310 acres aforesaid, and on the northeast by land originally granted John Munro for 150 acres, but on a resurvey found to contain the said surplus of 50 acres, northwest by Thomas Flin's, southeast by land now the property of the grantee originally surveyed and granted John Holms for 400 acres, but which on a resurvey is found to contain only 345 acres part of which said surplus land is in lieu of the deficiency of 55 acres wanted in the tract of 400 acres as aforesaid.

****

McIntosh, Lachlan
300 acres in St. Andrew Parish

Granted on June 7, 1774   Grant Book I, page 1038

300 acres bounded on the west by Donald Ross, south by Peter Nephew, north by land supposed to be George McIntosh's and on the east partly by vacant land at the time of the survey.

****

McIntosh, Lachlan
100 acres in St. Andrew Parish

Granted on August 2, 1774   Grant Book M, page 222

100 acres bounded on the west and northwest by Thomas King, Norman McDonald and James Westley and northeast by Donald McDonald.

****

McIntosh, Lachlan
120 acres in St. Andrew Parish

Granted on November 1, 1774   Grant Book M, page 693

120 acres bounded on the east and southeast by William McIntosh and on the southwest by the said Lachlan McIntosh.

****

McIntosh, Lachlan
350 acres in St. Andrew Parish

Granted on November 1, 1774   Grant Book M, page 694

350 acres situate on Cathead Creek and bounded on all sides by vacant land.

****

McIntosh, Lachlan
150 acres in St. Andrew Parish

Surveyed on October 4, 1765   Plat Book C, page 444
Granted on November 1, 1774   Grant Book M, page 695

150 acres bounded on the southeast by John Gray, as shown by the plat of survey.

****

McIntosh, Lachlan
250 acres in St. Andrew Parish

Granted on November 1, 1774   Grant Book M, page 696

250 acres bounded on the southwest by William McIntosh and vacant land, northwest by Governor James Wright and Darien Common and on all other sides by the said Lachlan McIntosh.

****

McIntosh, Lachlan, Sr.
300 acres in St. Andrew Parish

Granted on October 4, 1774   Grant Book M, page 578

300 acres bounded on the north and east by Daniel Demetre,
west by Levi and Benjamin Sheftall and on the south by
marshes.

****

McIntosh, Lachlan
432 acres in St. Andrew Parish

Surveyed on November 15, 1761   Plat Book C, page 260

432 acres bounded on the northeast by Cat Head Creek and on
the southeast by the Altamaha River.

****

McIntosh, Roderick
100 acres in St. Andrew Parish

Surveyed on January 10, 1771   Plat Book C, page 272
Granted on March 5, 1771   Grant Book I, page 272

100 acres bounded on the northeast by land of the said
grantee. The plat of survey shows this to be bounded on
the northeast by John McIntosh.

****

McIntosh, Roderick
50 acres in St. Andrew Parish

Granted on February 7, 1775   Grant Book M, page 1026

50 acres bounded on the north and east by salt marshes of the
Sapelo River and south and west by Philip Delegall.

****

McIntosh, William
50 acres in St. Andrew Parish

Surveyed on December 5, 1759   Plat Book C, page 239
Granted on April 13, 1761   Grant Book D, page 335

50 acres bounded on the southeast by William McIntosh, as shown on the plat of survey.

****

McIntosh, William
200 acres in St. Andrew Parish

Granted on February 3, 1767   Grant Book F, page 68

200 acres bounded on the north by Cathead Creek, southwest by Robert Baillie, and on every other side by land vacant which said tract was heretofore ordered to and surveyed for William McKay.

****

McIntosh, William
100 acres in St. Andrew Parish

Granted on November 1, 1768   Grant Book G, page 214

100 acres bounded on the west by Sir Patrick Houstoun and on the north by the widow Grant.

****

McIntosh, William
50 acres in St. Andrew Parish

Surveyed on August 1, 1769   Plat Book C, page 213
Granted on September 5, 1769   Grant Book H, page 28

50 acres bounded on the northeast by land of the said grantee and on the south by George Threadcraft.

****

McIntosh, William
50 acres in St. Andrew Parish

Granted on May 7, 1771   Granted Book H, page 57

50 acres bounded at the time of the survey by land laid out for Captain John Gray and on all other sides by land vacant.

****

McIntosh, William
50 acres in St. Andrew Parish

Surveyed on January 21, 1769   Plat Book C, page 234
Granted on June 7, 1774   Grant Book H, page 127

50 acres bounded on the south by Alexander McDonald and on
all other sides by vacant land at the time of the survey, the
same having been heretofore ordered to and surveyed for
Alexander McDonald. Plat of survey show tract ordered to
William McIntosh on March 5, 1771.

                          ****

McIntosh, William
100 acres in St. Andrew Parish

Surveyed on January 24, 1771   Plat Book C, page 273
Granted on July 2, 1771   Grant Book I, page 368

100 acres bounded on the south by Minis, southwest by George
Threadercroft and north by Brydie. Plat of survey shows
tract bounded on the north by Rudy.

                          ****

McIntosh, William
250 acres in St. Andrew Parish

Surveyed on April 26, 1773   Plat Book C, page 294 & 403
Granted on August 2, 1774   Grant Book M, page 220

250 acres bounded on the north by vacant marsh, east by ___Bird,
and on all other sides by William McIntosh. The tract is surplus
of a tract formerly surveyed for Captain John McIntosh, deceased.

                          ****

McIntosh, William
150 acres in St. Andrew Parish

Surveyed on February 6, 1773   Plat Book C, page 289
Granted on August 2, 1774   Grant Book M, page 221

150 acres bounded on the southwest, southeast and northwest by
said William McIntosh and northeast by vacant marsh. The tract
is surplus land found on a resurvey of a tract he purchased of
John McIntosh.

                          ****

McIntosh, William
400 acres in St. Andrew Parish

Granted on September 6, 1774   Grant Book M, page 345

400 acres bounded on the west by George McIntosh, southeast by George McIntosh and George Gray, southwest by Lachlan McIntosh, Robert McIntosh and George McIntosh.

****

McIntosh, William
500 acres in St. Andrew Parish

Granted on September 9, 1774   Grant Book M, page 352

500 acres on Black Island and bounded on all sides by the Altamaha River and branches and creeks of the same. Black Island contains 700 acres and 200 acres have already been granted.

****

McIntosh, William
300 acres in St. Andrew Parish

Granted on November 1, 1774   Grant Book M, page 700

300 acres bounded on the northeast by a creek and marshes and on the southeast by William McIntosh.

****

McIntosh, William
200 acres in St. Andrew Parish

Granted on November 1, 1774   Grant Book M, page 701

200 acres bounded on the southeast by Sapelo River and marshes, southwest by Roderick McKay, northwest by John McIntosh, John McIntosh and William McIntosh's ricefield and northeast by Mr. Bird.

****

McIntosh, William
94 acres in St. Andrew Parish

Surveyed on June 16, 1773   Plat Book C, page 291

94 acres bounded on the west by George Thredcraft and on all other sides by William McIntosh.

****

McKay, Angus
100 acres in St. Andrew Parish

Surveyed on April 28, 1769 Plat Book C, page 229
Granted on December 5, 1769 Grant Book G, page 476

100 acres bounded on the east by Edmund Harrold and Mrs. McCulloch. Plat shows that the tract is bounded on the west by James Munroe and south by Cat Head Creek.

****

McKay, Angus
150 acres in St. Andrew Parish

Surveyed on August 29, 1771 Plat Book C, page 281
Granted on April 7, 1772 Grant Book I, page 564

150 acres bounded on the southeast by George McDonald and Angus McIntosh.

****

McKay, Angus
150 acres in St. Andrew Parish

Granted on September 6, 1774 Grant Book M, page 346

150 acres bounded on the northwest by Joseph Gibbons, Samuel Hestings and James Heart, southeast by Angus McKay and Donald McDonald and southwest by Benjamin Farley.

****

McKay, Angus
100 acres in St. Andrew Parish

Surveyed on March 17, 1772 Plat Book C, page 291

100 acres bounded on the southwest by George McIntosh, northeast by land laid out for Angus McKay and on the southeast by Canadas and George McDonald.

****

McKay, Elizabeth Ann
450 acres in St. Andrew Parish

Granted on February 7, 1775   Grant Book M, page 1023

450 acres bounded on the east by William Clark and Daniel McIntosh and on the northwest by Robert Baillie.

****

McKay, Elizabeth Ann
50 acres in St. Andrew Parish

Granted on February 7, 1775   Grant Book M, page 1024

50 acres bounded on the east by a south branch of Sapelo River, northwest by Robert Baillie and southwest by Roderick McKay.

****

McKay, James
500 acres in St. Andrew Parish

Surveyed on April 19, 1769   Plat Book C, page 251
Granted on August 1, 1769   Grant Book G, page 390

500 acres bounded on all sides by vacant land.

****

McKay, James
150 acres in St. Andrew Parish

Surveyed on June 21, 1769   Plat Book C, page 253
Granted on April 7, 1772   Grant Book I, page 565

150 acres bounded on the southeast by the said grantee, on the northwest by James Read and on the southwest by Mary Milton.

****

McKay, James
300 acres in St. Andrew Parish

Granted on April 7, 1772   Grant Book I, page 566

300 acres bounded on the southwest by the Altamaha River, northwest by William Herbert and on the northeast by Marmaduke Perry, George Moore and Samuel Lewis.

****

McKay, James
310 acres in St. Andrew Parish

Surveyed on October 16, 1771   Plat Book C, page 277
Granted on May 5, 1772   Grant Book I, page 597

310 acres bounded on the south by the said grantee. The plat of survey states that this is St. David Parish but the author believes this to be incorrect.

****

McKay, James
300 acres in St. Andrew Parish

Surveyed on May 11, 1772   Plat Book C, page 288
Granted on June 2, 1772   Grant Book I, page 622

300 acres bounded on the east by the said grantee and on the west by Moses Way.

****

McKay, James
150 acres in St. Andrew Parish

Granted on December 6, 1774   Grant Book M, page 815

150 acres bounded on the east by the said James McKay and vacant land.

****

McKay, James
500 acres in St. Andrew Parish

Surveyed on April 21, 1756   Plat Book C, page 262

500 acres bounded on the west by Thomas Smith and on the east by James McKay.

****

McKay, James
500 acres in St. Andrew Parish

Surveyed on May 23, 1770   Plat Book C, page 253

500 acres bounded on the south and west by the Altamaha River,
north by John Jones and John Witherspoon and east by D.
Witherspoon and vacant land.

****

McKay, Patrick
1126 acres in St. Andrew Parish

Granted on February 7, 1775   Grant Book M, page 1028

1126 acres bounded on the north by Daniel McKenzie and on
the east by William Clark.

****

McKay, Robert
200 acres in St. Andrew Parish

Surveyed on May 4, 1769   Plat Book C, page 264
Granted on July 4, 1769   Grant Book G, page 364

200 acres bounded on the north by Hugh Clark and on the
southwest by Abigail Minis and Donald McKay.

****

McKay, Robert
100 acres in St. Andrew Parish

Granted on February 4, 1772   Grant Book I, page 512

100 acres bounded on the east by Stephens.

****

McKay, William
200 acres in St. Andrew Parish

Surveyed on January 1, 1762   Plat Book C, page 238

200 acres bounded on the southwest by Robert Baillie, southeast
by Robert Baillie and northeast by Cathead Creek.

****

McKeethen, Alexander
400 acres in St. Andrew Parish

Surveyed on July 30, 1760   Plat Book C, page 224

400 acres of fresh marsh bounded by Alagator Creek and The
North River that goes to Darien.

****

McKenzie, Alexander
100 acres in St. Andrew Parish

Surveyed on May 27, 1757   Plat Book C, page 437
Granted on May 1, 1759   Grant Book B, page 136

100 acres in the district of S pelo bounded on the northeast
by John McIntosh and southeast by Thomas Bates.

****

McKenzie, Alexander
150 acres in St. Andrew Parish

Surveyed on January 29, 1761   Plat Book C, page 408
Granted on December 7, 1762   Grant Book D, page 252

150 acres bounded on the southwest by James Monroe, northwest
by Norman McDonald and Daniel Rose. The plat of survey states
that the McDonlad and Rose land was 50 acre lots in old Darien.

****

McKenzie, Donald
200 acres in St. Andrew Parish

Surveyed on October 11, 1764   Plat Book C, page 233
Granted on April 7, 1767   Grant Book F, page 195

200 acres bounded on the east by (?) Clark and on the north
by the said Donald McKenzie. Plat of survey shows that on
the east it was bounded by William Clark and on the north
by Donald McKenzie.

****

McKenzie, William
100 acres in St. Andrew Parish

100 acres bounded on the west by a public road.

****

McKitcthen, Alexander
350 acres in St. Andrew Parish

Surveyed on August 14, 1760   Plat Book C, page 219

350 acres bounded on the southeast and east by salt marsh and on the west by Samuel Smith.

****

McKinnen, Charles William
5000 acres in St. Andrew Parish

Surveyed on November 29, 1771   Plat Book C, page 282
Granted on March 3, 1772   Grant Book I, page 533

5000 acres bounded on the southwest by the Altamaha River, northwest by Inigo Jones, southwest by Samuel Miller, Grey Elliott, James Read, Mary Molton, James McKay, James Maxwell, Joseph Butler and Joseph Gibbons.

****

McKintosh, George
112 acres in St. Andrew Parish

Surveyed on September 22, 1765   Plat Book C, page 255
Granted on September 2, 1766   Grant Book E, page 365

112 acres bounded on the south and east by Hugh Morrison and -----Gray and on the north by the said George McKintosh.

****

McKintosh, George
150 acres in St. Andrew Parish

Surveyed on September 27, 1766   Plat Book C, page 237
Granted on November 4, 1766   Grant Book E, page 397

150 acres bounded on the southeast by Hugh Morrison and on the east by the said George McKintosh.

****

McKintosh, George
250 acres in St. Andrew Parish

Surveyed on August 12, 1766   Plat Book C, page 237
Granted on November 4, 1766   Grant Book E, page 399

250 acres bounded on the southeast by marhses of Sapelo
River, east by George Gray and west by John Gray and the
said George McKintosh.

****

McKintosh, Lachlan
500 acres in St. Andrew Parish

Surveyed on July 21, 1758   Plat Book C, page 261
Granted on August 7, 1759   Grant Book B, page 176

500 acres on an island in the Altamaha River and bounded on
the south by the said river, northeast by Cathead Creek and
northwest by lands vacant.

****

McKintosh, Lachlan
250 acres in St. Andrew Parish

Surveyed on August 15, 1766   Plat Book C, page 270
Granted on September 2, 1766   Grant Book E, page 367

250 acres being an island in the Altamaha River and bounded
on the north by marshes of the said river and on every other
side by marshes and creeks leading from the river.

****

McKintosh, Lachlan
150 acres in St. Andrew Parish

Granted on November 4, 1766   Grant Book E, page 396

150 acres bounded on the southeast by Captain John Gray,
deceased.

****

McLeod, Catharine, James and John
300 acres in St. Andrew Parish

Granted on August 2, 1774   Grant Book M, page 231

300 acres bounded on the east by unknown land and on all other sides by vacant land.

                          ****

McLeod, James, Catherine and John
300 acres in St. Andrew Parish

Granted on August 2, 1774   Grant Book M, page 231

300 acres bounded on the east by unknown land and on all other sides by vacant land.

                          ****

McLeod, John, Catherine and James
300 acres in St. Andrew Parish

Granted on August 2, 1774   Grant Book M, page 231

300 acres bounded on the east by unknown land and on all other sides by vacant land.

                          ****

McLeod, John
100 acres in St. Andrew Parish

Surveyed on December 17, 1769   Plat Book C, page 217 & 409

100 acres bounded on the northwest by George McIntosh, southeast by Alexander Gray and southwest by Hugh Morrison.

                          ****

McLeod, Murdock
150 acres in St. Andrew Parish

Granted on July 7, 1761   Grant Book D, page 75

150 acres bounded on all sides by vacant land.

                          ****

McLeod, Roderick
200 acres in St. Andrew Parish

Surveyed on January 23, 1767   Plat Book C, page 226
Granted on February 3, 1767   Grant Book F, page 69

200 acres bounded on the south by the Altamaha River, west by
Cathead Creek and northwest by Lachaln McIntosh.

                              ****

McLoud, Murdock
100 acres in St. Andrew Parish

Granted on February 7, 1758   Grant Book A, page 563

100 acres in the district of Darien and bounded on the north
by ------McLoud.

                              ****

Melton, Mary, widow
300 acres in St. Andrew Parish

Granted on February 6, 1770   Grant Book G, page 525

300 acres bounded on the southeast by James Read and on the
northwest partly by James Read.

                              ****

Middleton, John
300 acres in St. Andrew Parish

Surveyed on June 23, 1761   Plat Book C, page 248
Granted on July 5, 1763   Grant Book D, page 309

300 acres bounded on all sides by vacant land.

                              ****

Miller, Robert
500 acres in St. Andrew Parish

Surveyed on March 12, 1761   Plat Book C, page 261 & 409
Granted on February 5, 1765   Grant Book E, page 104

500 acres bounded on the southwest by the Altamaha River and
on all other sides by vacant land.

                              ****

Miller, Robert
500 acres in St. Andrew Parish

Surveyed on November 1, 1761   Plat Book C, page 243 & 409
Granted on February 5, 1765   Grant Book E, page105

500 acres bounded on the southwest by the Altamaha River and
on the southeast by Robert Miller.

****

Miller, Samuel
500 acres in St. Andrew Parish

Surveyed on April 26, 1769   Plat Book C, page 262
Granted on August 1, 1869   Grant Book G, page 392

 500 acres bounded on the southeast by James Reid and vacant
land, according to the plat of survey.

****

Miller, Samuel
400 acres in St. Andrew Parish

Surveyed on May 3, 1771   Plat Book C, page 272
Granted on June 5, 1771   Grant Book I, page 344

400 acres bounded on the northeast and partly on the northwest
by land of the said grantee and on all other sides by vacant
land.

****

Miller, Samuel
100 acres in St. Andrew Parish

Surveyed on May 4, 1771   Plat Book C, page 272
Granted on June 5, 1771   Grant Book I, page 345

100 acres bounded partly on the northeast by land of the
said grantee.

****

Miller, Samuel
100 acres in St. Andrew Parish

Surveyed on May 4, 1771   Plat Book C, page 272
Granted on October 1, 1771   Grant Book I, page 435

100 acres bounded partly on the southeast and partly on the
southwest by the said grantee.

****

Mills, Thomas
100 acres in St. Andrew Parish

Surveyed on December 27, 1759   Plat Book C, page 224 & 408
Granted on November 27, 1761   Grant Book C, page 339

100 acres bounded on all sides by vacant land.

****

Milton, Mary
300 acres in St. Andrew Parish

Surveyed on April 26, 1769   Plat Book C, page 264

300 acres bounded on the northwest and southeast by James
Read.

****

Minis, Abigail, Widow
500 acres in St. Andrew Parish

Surveyed on May 1757   Plat Book C, page 443
Granted on December 6, 1757   Grant Book A, page 574

500 acres in the District of Sapelo and bounded on the southeast by Daniel Mackay.

****

Monroe, Donald
100 acres in St. Andrew Parish

Surveyed on August 8, 1759   Plat Book C, page 403
Granted on October 2, 1759   Grant Book C, page 231

100 acres bounded on the west by Donald Kennedy and east by
Stuart.

****

Monroe, James
150 acres in St. Andrew Parish

Granted on December 4, 1759   Grant Book B, page 366

150 acres bounded on the south by Cathead Creek and on the west by Sir Patrick Houstoun.

****

Monroe, John
155 acres in St. Andrew Parish

Granted on July 1, 1760   Grant Book B, page 483

155 acres bounded on the east by John Holmes, southwest by Cathead Creek and the land of Edmund Harold.

****

Moore, George
200 acres in St. Andrew Parish

Surveyed on December 24, 1760   Plat Book C, page 221 & 408
Granted on November 2, 1762   Grant Book D, page 231

200 acres bounded on the northwest by Samuel Tomlinson and southeast by Samuel Lewis.

****

Moore, George
100 acres in St. Andrew Parish

Surveyed on February 8, 1771   Plat Book C, page 280
Granted on January 19, 1773   Grant Book I, page 866

100 acres bounded on the north by William Mills.

****

Moore, George
100 acres in St. Andrew Parish

Surveyed on December 21, 1770   Plat Book C, page 444

100 acres bounded on all sides by vacant land.

****

Moore, Giles
150 acres in St. Andrew Parish

Surveyed on May 31, 1768   Plat Book C, page 263
Granted on November 6, 1770   Grant Book I, page 188

150 acres bounded on all sides by vacant land.

****

Morel, John
1500 acres in St. Andrew Parish

Surveyed on October 21, 1772   Plat Book C, page 286
Granted on May 4, 1773   Grant Book I, page 986

1500 acres bounded on the east by Joseph Woodruff, William
Spencer and Jane Bourquin, on the north by Clement Martin,
on the west by James Luna, Joseph Butler, Joseph Gibbons
and Anthony Stokes.

****

Morell, John
400 acres in St. Andrew Parish

Surveyed on March 25, 1773   Plat Book C, page 289
Granted on April 6, 1773   Grant Book I, page 956

400 acres bounded on the south by the Altamaha River, east
by Alexander Thomson, west by Charles William Mackinnen and
north by Anthony Stokes.

****

Morrison, Hugh
250 acres in St. Andrew Parish

Granted on July 4, 1758   Grant Book B, page 464

250 acres in the District of Sapelo and bounded on the southeast by Hugh Clark.

****

Moza, Charles
100 acres in St. Andrew Parish

Granted on April 4, 1775   Grant Book M, page 1107

100 acres bounded on the northeast by John Gasper Starkey, and on the northwest by John Stuart and John D'honours.

****

Munro, Simon
300 acres in St. Andrew Parish

Granted on November 1, 1774   Grant Book M, page 703

300 acres bounded on the southwest by Angus McIntosh, west by Angus McKay and vacant land, east by Joseph Merrett and Thomas Morris and north by Simon Munro.

****

Munro, Simon
500 acres in St. Andrew Parish

Granted on November 1, 1774   Grant Book M, page 704

500 acres bounded on the south by Simon Munro and on the east by Captain Morris and Simon Munro.

****

Munro, Simon and Roger Kelsall
200 acres in St. Andrew Parish

Granted on February 2, 1768   Grant Book G, page 25

200 acres bounded on the northwest by John Lawson, on the southeast by Samuel Sanders and on the southwest by the Altamaha River. The tract was originally ordered to John Perkins.

****

Munroe, James
50 acres in St. Andrew Parish

Surveyed on October 12, 1766   Plat Book C, page 262
Granted on March 7, 1769   Grant Book H, page 17

50 acres bounded on the southeast by James Munroe and on the southwest by Murdoch McCloud.

****

Munroe, Simon and Roger Kelsall
300 acres in St. Andrew Parish

Surveyed on February 26, 1762   Plat Book C, page 118

300 acres bounded on the southwest by the Altamaha River,
northwest by William ,cKormack and vacant land, and southeast
by Robert Miller.

****

Nephew, Peter
200 acres in St. Andrew Parish

Granted on July 3, 1770   Grant Book I, page 54

200 acres bounded on the south by John Grant, north by Donald
Rose, east partly by land vacant and partly by the said
Peter Nephew and on every other side by vacant land.

****

Nephew, Peter
250 acres in St. Andrew Parish

Granted on August 7, 1770   Grant Book I, page 77

250 acres bounded on all sides by vacant land.

****

Nephew, Peter
100 acres in St. Andrew Parish

Granted on September 6, 1774   Grant Book M, page 365

100 acres bounded on the west by John Grant, northwest by the
said Peter Nephew and north by James Westly.

****

Nephew, Peter
250 acres in St. Andrew Parish

Granted on November 1, 1774   Grant Book M, page 714

250 acres bounded on the south by the said Peter Nephew.

****

Norman, Baruch
150 acres in St. Andrew Parish

Granted on July 1, 1760   Grant Book D, page 48

150 acres bounded on the west by Strong Ashmore.

****

Oates, Jacob
200 acres in St. Andrew Parish

Granted on July 7, 1772   Grant Book I, page 680

200 acres bounded on the southeast by James Sucend and James
Houstoun.

****

Oates, John
500 acres in St. Andrew Parish

Granted on December 5, 1769   Grant Book G, page 478

500 acres bounded on all sides by vacant land.

****

Oates, John
100 acres in St. Andrew Parish

Surveyed on January 27, 1771   Plat Book C, page 275
Granted on October 1, 1771   Grant Book I, page 437

100 acres originally surveyed for Charles Mahanahan, thence
ordered on July 2, 1771 to John Oates.

****

Oates, John
300 acres in St. Andrew Parish

Granted on October 4, 1774   Grant Book M, page 587

300 acres bounded on the south by land reserved for John Bowman
and vacant land, west by George Johnson Turner and north by
vacant and surveyed land.

****

Oates, John (in trust for Lamar Waters)
300 acres in St. Andrew Parish

Surveyed on May 21, 1770   Plat Book C, page 415

300 acres bounded on the east by David Dicks and on the north
by John Oates.

****

Odensal, Charles
350 acres in St. Andrew Parish

Granted on April 3, 1770   Grant Book G, page 584

350 acres bounded on all sides by vacant land.

****

Odensall, Charles
300 acres in St. Andrew Parish

Granted on April 3, 1770   Grant Book G, page 585

300 acres bounded on the southeast by Brice McCleland.

****

Osgood, John
150 acres in St. Andrew Parish

Granted on December 4, 1770   Grant Book I, page 223

150 acres bounded on all sides by vacant land.

****

Osgood, John (Reverend)
200 acres in St. Andrew Parish

Granted on May 5, 1772   Grant Book I, page 599

200 acres bounded on all sides by vacant land.

****

Osgood, John (Reverend)
200 acres in St. Andrew Parish

Granted on May 5, 1772   Grant Book I, page 600

200 acres bounded on all sides by vacant land.

****

Osgood, John, Jr.
150 acres in St. Andrew Parish

Granted on September 6, 1774   Grant Book M, page 366

150 acres bounded on the southeast by Abraham Lewis and on the northeast by John Osgood.

****

Osgood, Josiah, Jr.
250 acres in St. Andrew Parish

Surveyed on April 1, 1761   Plat Book C, page 415
Granted on January 5, 1762   Grant Book D, page 5

250 acres bounded on the northeast by John Stewart.

****

Osgood, Josiah, Jr.
300 acres in St. Andrew Parish

Granted on April 3, 1770   Grant Book G, page 583

300 acres bounded on the northeast by Josiah Osgood.

****

Oswell, Joseph
300 acres in St. Andrew Parish

Granted on March 1, 1768   Grant Book G, page 58

300 acres bounded on the north by James Andrew and on the east by Ann Andrew.

****

Oswell, Joseph
300 acres in St. Andrew Parish

Granted on August 1, 1769   Grant Book G, page 394

300 acres bounded on the south by Stephen Clark.

****

Patton, John
300 acres in St. Andrew Parish

Granted on October 4, 1774   Grant Book M, page 592

300 acres bounded on all sides by vacant land.

****

Peacock, Thomas
150 acres in St. Andrew Parish

Granted on July 1, 1760   Grant Book D, page 2

150 acres bounded on the west by Palmer Golding.

****

Peacock, Thomas
150 acres in St. Andrew Parish

Granted on January 1, 1771   Grant Book I, page 241

150 acres bounded on all sides by vacant land.

****

Peacock, Thomas
300 acres in St. Andrew Parish

Granted on February 7, 1775   Grant Book M, page 1042

300 acres bounded on the east by Samuel Miller.

****

Peacock, William
200 acres in St. Andrew Parish

Granted on December 4, 1770   Grant Book I, page 225

200 acres bounded partly on the southeast and partly on the
northeast by Thomas Kelly and on all other sides by vacant.

****

Pearce, Edmund
150 acres in St. Andrew Parish

Granted on October 2, 1764   Grant Book E, page 44

150 acres bounded on the northwest by John Stacey and southwest by John Perkins.

****

Perkins, John
500 acres in St. Andrew Parish

Surveyed on November 7, 1753   Plat Book C, page 396
Granted on May 15, 1756   Grant Book A, page 222

500 acres in the District of Darien, known as Hopewell and
bounded on the southwest by Buchanan and on the east by the
marshes of Darien River.

****

Perry, Marmaduke
250 acres in St. Andrew Parish

Surveyed on August 3, 1759   Plat Book C, page 418

250 acres bounded on the southwest by Lewis Creek.

****

Piercy, Joseph
200 acres in St. Andrew Parish

Granted on November 1, 1774   Grant Book M, page 719

200 acres bounded on the north by James Grant and on the
east by salt marshes.

****

Piercy, Joseph
200 acres in St. Andrew Parish

Surveyed on October 26, 1758   Plat Book C, page 418

200 acres bounded on the east by marshes of Sapelo, west by
marsh and north by William Thomas Harris.

****

Ponsheer, Jean
100 acres in St. Andrew Parish

Granted on September 6, 1768   Grant Book G, page 188

100 acres bounded on the east by Hugh Clark and John McDonald, northeast by Hugh Morrison and northwest by Ann McKintosh.

****

Poulson, John
150 acres in St. Andrew Parish

Granted August 5, 1766   Grant Book E, page 342

150 acres bounded on the southeast by a creek that runs into the Sapelo River and on the southwest by John Poulson.

****

Poulson, John
150 acres in St. Andrew Parish

Granted on August 5, 1766   Grant Book E, page 343

150 acres bounded on the southeast by a creek that runs into Sapelo River and on the northeast by the said John Poulson.

****

Pryce, Charles, Jr.
500 acres in St. Andrew Parish

Granted on August 4, 1772   Grant Book I, page 711

500 acres bounded partly on the northwest by William Telfair and on all other sides by vacant land.

****

Quarterman, Thomas
100 acres in St. Andrew Parish

Granted on October 6, 1767   Grant Book F, page 392

100 acres bounded on the south by the said Thomas Quarterman.

****

Quarterman, Thomas
170 acres in St. Andrew Parish

Granted on January 3, 1775   Grant Book M, page 927

170 acres bounded on the north by William Jones and on all
other sides by the said Thomas Quarterman.

****

Quarterman, Thomas
130 acres in St. Andrew Parish

Granted on January 3, 1775   Grant Book M, page 928

130 acres bounded on the northeast by vacant land and on all
other sides by the said Thomas Quarterman.

****

Read, James
500 acres in St. Andrew Parish

Granted on March 6, 1770   Grant Book G, page 562

500 acres bounded on all sides by vacant land.

****

Ready, Thomas
150 acres in St. Andrew Parish

Granted on February 7, 1775   Grant Book M, page 1043

150 acres bounded on the northeast by John McDonald, west by
Angus Clark and southeast by John Houstoun.

****

Reddy, Thomas
150 acres in St. Andrew Parish

Granted on August 1, 1769   Grant Book G, page 395

150 acres bounded on the north by William McKintosh and vacant
land, west by George Threadcraft, south by vacant land and
east by Alexander McKenzie.

****

Rian, John
100 acres in St. Andrew Parish

Granted on June 6, 1769   Grant Book G, page 343

100 acres bounded on the north by Robert Baillie, south by
William Kenedy and east by Ann McIntosh.

                         ****

Rian, William
250 acres in St. Andrew Parish

Granted on February 5, 1771   Grant Book I, page 256

250 acres bounded on the southwest by land of Grantee William
Jones, and on the northeast by the north branch of Sapelo River.

                         ****

Richardson, Samuel
300 acres in St. Andrew Parish

Surveyed on February 3, 1760   Plat Book C, page 433

300 acres bounded on all sides by vacant land.

                         ****

Riddock, Collin
400 acres in St. Andrew Parish

Granted on December 4, 1770   Grant Book I, page 228

400 acres bounded on the southeast by the Altamaha River and
northeast by Thomas Carter.

                         ****

Ried, Thomas
500 acres in St. Andrew Parish

Granted on September 6, 1774   Grant Book M, page 400

500 acres bounded on all sides by vacant land.

                         ****

Rivers, John
455 acres in St. Andrew Parish

Granted on November 1, 1774   Grant Book M, page 721

455 acres bounded on the southwest by Captain Andrew Maybank,
northwest by Stephen Williams, northwest by Daniel Sullivant
and Thomas Sullivant and southeast by Thomas Coxe.

****

Rolland, Christian, widow
200 acres in St. Andrew Parish

Granted on May 3, 1768   Grant Book G, page 108

200 acres bounded on the southeast by George McKintosh.

****

Rose, Daniel
100 acres in St. Andrew Parish

Granted on April 5, 1763   Grant Book D, page 299

100 acres bounded on the north by the said Daniel Rose and
on the west by a savannah.

****

Ross, Donald
200 acres in St. Andrew Parish

Granted on October 2, 1759   Grant Book B, page 197

200 acres in the District of Darien and bounded on all sides
by vacant land.

****

Ross, Hugh
250 acres in St. Andrew Parish

Granted on February 7, 1758   Grant Book A, page 608

250 acres in the District of Darien and bounded on the northwest by Daniel McDonald and on the northeast by Angus Mackay.

****

Ross, Hugh
50 acres in St. Andrew Parish

Surveyed on July 20, 1761   Plat Book C, page 421
Granted on May 21, 1762   Grant Book D, page 95

50 acres bounded on the south by Samuel Fulton, east by Daniel
Clark and John Gray, north by John Grant and west by George
Kid and Samuel Fulton. Plat also show McColler on the east
and south.

****

Ross, Hugh
42 acres in St. Andrew Parish

Surveyed on July 11, 1759   Plat Book C, page 421

42 acres bounded on the north by marshes of South Newport
River, southeast by Donald Munroe and southwest by Donald
Kennedy.

****

Sallins, Peter
150 acres in St. Andrew Parish

Surveyed on June 8, 1770   Plat Book C, page 308
Granted on January 1, 1771   Grant Book I, page 243

150 acres bounded partly on the northwest by James McKay and
partly by Thomas Smith, northeast by John Martin, southwest
by Sarah Spencer and southeast by vacant land.

****

Sallins, Peter
250 acres in St. Andrew Parish

Surveyed on June 9, 1772   Plat Book C, page 351
Granted on January 19, 1773   Grant Book I, page 885

250 acres bounded on the southwest by the said grantee.

****

Sallin, Peter
110 acres in St. Andrew Parish

Granted on January 19, 1773   Grant Book I, page 886

110 acres bounded on the northwest by the said grantee.

****

Sallins, Peter
500 acres in St. Andrew Parish

Granted on January 19, 1773   Grant Book I, page 887

500 acres bounded partly on the southwest and partly on the northwest by John McCulloch and on all other sides by vacant.

****

Sallins, Peter
100 acres in St. Andrew Parish

Granted on January 19, 1773   Grant Book I, page 888

100 acres bounded on the south by John McCulloch and the said grantee.

****

Sallins, Peter
100 acres in St. Andrew Parish

Surveyed on June 9, 1772   Plat Book C, page 350
Granted on January 19, 1773   Grant Book I, page 889

100 acres bounded on the northeast by John McCulloch.

****

Sanders, Samuel
150 acres in St. Andrew Parish

Surveyed on March 11, 1761   Plat Book C, page 320
Granted on January 19, 1773   Grant Book I, page 860

150 acres originally surveyed for Samuel Sanders thence ordered to Lewis Johnson and Alexander Wylly. Bounded on the southwest by the Altamaha River.

****

Senior, George
300 acres in St. Andrew Parish

Surveyed on August 3, 1759   Plat Book C, page 296
Granted on February 5, 1760   Grant Book B, page 372

300 acres bounded on all sides by vacant land.

                    ****

Sheftal, Benjamin
200 acres in St. Andrew Parish

Granted on February 5, 1760   Grant Book B, page 352

200 acres in the District of Sapelo, bounded on the east by
Daniel Demetre, deceased, north by vacant land and on all
other sides by marshes of the South Newport River.

                    ****

Sheftal, Levi
150 acres in St. Andrew Parish

Surveyed on April 26, 1761   Plat Book C, page 426
Granted on May 3, 1763   Grant Book D, page 304

150 acres bounded on the west by Johnson's marsh and south by
land of the said Levi Sheftal.

                    ****

Sheftall, Levi
100 acres in St. Andrew Parish

Surveyed on March 7, 1758   Plat Book C, page 303
Granted on May 1, 1759   Grant Book C, page 223

100 acres bounded on the south by Benjamin Sheftall, east by
vacant land and on all other sides by marshes of South New-
Port River.

                    ****

Sheftall, Levi
150 acres in St. Andrew Parish

Surveyed on April 26, 1761   Plat Book C, page 303

150 acres bounded on the south by Levi Sheftall and west by Johnson and marsh.

****

Sherrard, Alexander
200 acres in St. Andrew Parish

Surveyed on October 12, 1769   Plat Book C, page 323
Granted on May 1, 1770   Grant Book I, page 10

200 acres bounded on the southwest by the Altamaha River and on the southeast by Matthew Frederick.

****

Sherrod, Alexander
200 acres in St. Andrew Parish

Surveyed on June 10, 1769   Plat Book C, page 308

200 acres bounded on the southwest by the Altamaha River.

****

Shruder, Thomas
500 acres in St. Andrew Parish

Surveyed on October 17, 1772   Plat Book C, page 349
Granted on January 5, 1773   Grant Book I, page 836

500 acres bounded on all sides by vacant land.

****

Shruder, Thomas
300 acres in St. Andrew Parish

Granted on August 2, 1774   Grant Book M, page 249

300 acres bounded on the northwest and northeast by the said Thomas Shruder.

****

Shute, John
200 acres in St. Andrew Parish

Surveyed on February 9, 1762   Plat Book C, page 314
Granted on May 21, 1762   Grant Book D, page 121

200 acres at the South Newport River on a branch of the
Mortar Swamp and bounded on the north and east by the said
John Shute, west and south by Joseph and Thomas Stevens and
southeast by John Stewart, Jr.

****

Shute, John
200 acres in St. Andrew Parish

Granted on May 21, 1762   Grant Book D, page 122

200 acres at South Newport on a branch of the Mortar Swamp
and bounded on the southand west by the said John Shute,
southeast by John Stewart, Jr., and northwest by land laid
out for John D'honeur.

****

Simmons, Elizabeth
600 acres in St. Andrew Parish

Surveyed on September 17, 1756   Plat Book C, page 295

600 acres bounded on the southeast by William Dunnom and
north by John Elliott and Andrew Way.

****

Simpson, Archibald
700 acres in St. Andrew Parish

Surveyed on June 28, 1761   Plat Book C, page 329

700 acres bounded on the southwest by the Altamaha River, north
by John Jones, Swans Creek and Thomas King and north by Lewis
Creek. Includes an unnamed island, acreage not given in the
Altamaha River.

****

Simpson, John
150 acres in St. Andrew Parish

Granted on August 1, 1769   Grant Book G, page 396

150 acres bounded on all sides by vacant land.

Simpson, John
150 acres in St. Andrew Parish

Surveyed on May 30, 1770   Plat Book C, page 161
Granted on June 5, 1771   Grant Book I, page 353

150 acres bounded on the north by Samuel Lewis, Sr. and
Abraham Lewis, west by land of the said Samuel Lewis and
south by land of Isaac Lewis and the Altamaha River. It
was surveyed for Jacob Lewis, thence ordered to John Simpson on April 2, 1771. Granted to John Simpson.

****

Simpson, William
100 acres in St. Andrew Parish

Surveyed on November 5, 1772   Plat Book C, page 356

100 acres bounded on all sides by vacant land.

****

Smith, Nicholas
250 acres in St. Andrew Parish

Surveyed on November 24, 1768   Plat Book C, page 315
Granted on July 4, 1769   Grant Book G, page 372

250 acres bounded on the east by Gilbert Grant.

****

Southerland, Captain Patrick
500 acres in St. Andrew Parish

Granted on May 15, 1756   Grant Book A, page 102

500 acres on Sapelo River bounded on the west by Lieut. John
Gray, north by vacant lands and on all other sides by the
Sapelo River or the marshes of the same.

****

Spencer, Richard
176½ acres in St. Andrew Parish

Surveyed on February 13, 1760   Plat Book C, page 426
Granted on May 21, 1762   Grant Book D, page 112

Spencer, Sarah
300 acres in St. Andrew Parish

Surveyed on December 22, 1770   Plat Book C, page 345
Granted on July 2, 1771   Grant Book I, page 374

300 acres bounded on all sides by vacant land.

****

Spencer, Sarah
129 acres in St. Andrew Parish

Granted on July 5, 1774   Grant Book M, page 116

129 acres bounded on the west by Richard Spencer and William LeConts, southwest by Roger Kelsall, southeast by the said Roger Kelsall and northeast by Peter Sallen.

****

Spencer, Sarah, widow
150 acres in St. Andrew Parish

Surveyed on August 10, 1770   Plat Book C, page 327

150 acres bounded on the northeast by John Wynn and vacant land, southwest by Moses Way and northwest by Thomas Smith and Richard Spencer.

****

Spencer, William
600 acres in St. Andrew Parish

Granted on May 5, 1772   Grant Book I, page 606

600 acres bounded on the north by land surveyed for William Barnes.

****

Splat, Edward
600 acres in St. Andrew Parish

Surveyed on April 15, 1772   Plat Book C, page 358

600 acres bounded on all sides by vacant land.

****

Stacey. John
50 acres in St. Andrew Parish

Granted on December 3, 1760   Grant Book C. page 244

50 acres bounded on the northeast by John Perkins, southeast
by a creek and southwest by Thomas Camber.

****

Stacy, John
300 acres in St. Andrew Parish

Surveyed on May 21, 1768   Plat Book C, page 308
Granted on July 5, 1768   Grant Book G, page 143

300 acres bounded on the southeast by Edmund Peirce.

****

Stacy, John
250 acres in St. Andrew Parish

Surveyed on November 11, 1761   Plat Book C, page 318

250 acres bounded on all sides by vacant land.

****

Starkey, Gasper
250 acres in St. Andrew Parish

Surveyed on September 18, 1761   Plat Book C, page 426
Granted on May 21, 1762   Grant Book D, page 108

250 acres bounded on the southwest by land formerly laid out
for John Dehonneur and on the northeast by Benjamin Farley.

****

Starkey, Casper
100 acres in St. Andrew Parish

Surveyed on July 10, 1762   Plat Book C, page 300

100 acres bounded on the northeast by Casper Starkey and Farley.

****

Stevens, Joseph
300 acres in St. Andrew Parish

Granted on December 7, 1762   Grant Book D, page 260

Granted to Richard Baker in trust for Joseph and Thomas
Stevens.

****

Stevens, Samuel
500 acres in St. Andrew Parish

Granted on January 3, 1775   Grant Book M, page 944

500 acres bounded on the north by Hannah Bradwell, south by
William Bacon, west by Jane Stuart and vacant land.

****

Stevens, Thomas
300 acres in St. Andrew Parish

Surveyed on September 28, 1770   Plat Book C, page 341
Granted on April 2, 1771   Grant Book I, page 291

300 acres bounded on all sides by vacant land.

****

Stevens, Thomas
300 acres in St. Andrew Parish

Granted December 7, 1762   Grant Book D, page 260

Granted to Richard Baker in trust for Joseph and Thomas
Stevens.

****

Stewart, James
300 acres in St. Andrew Parish

Granted on June 2, 1772   Grant Book I, page 649

300 acres bounded on the east by land surveyed for the said
Grantee.

****

Stewart, James
150 acres in St. Andrew Parish

Surveyed on June 25, 1757   Plat Book C, page 334

150 acres bounded on the north by Daniel McIntosh.

****

Stewart, John
500 acres in St. Andrew Parish

Surveyed on September 18, 1755   Plat Book C, page 338
Granted on September 8, 1756   Grant Book A, page 199

500 acres on the Middle Branch of North Newport River and
bounded on the east by Joseph Bacon, west by William Baker.
Plat states that this is St. Andrew Parish.

****

Stewart, John
400 acres in St. Andrew Parish

Surveyed on March 23, 1771   Plat Book C, page 346
Granted on May 5, 1771   Grant Book I, page 607

400 acres bounded on the south by an old survey and vacant
land, east by Archibald McDonald and land surveyed for some
person unknown, and on all other sides by land vacant.

****

Stewart, John; Baker, Richard; Williams, Stephen, in trust
245 acres in St. Andrew Parish

Grante d on July 7, 1772   Granted Book I, page 656

245 acres bounded on the south by the Altamaha River , east
by Rutherford's Creek, north by Lewis Creek and west by a
creek called the Thoroughfare.

****

Stewart, John
200 acres in St. Andrew Parish

Surveyed on July 10, 1772   Plat Book C, page 359
Granted on September 6, 1774   Grant Book M, page 405

200 acres bounded on the northeast by land supposed to be surveyed for Dettonnor, northwest by the said John Stewart and southwest by Josiah Osgood.

****

Stewart, John
500 acres in St. Andrew Parish

Surveyed on January 25, 1757   Plat Book C, page 337

500 acres bounded on the southeast by Captain James McKay.

****

Stewart, John, Jr.
500 acres in St. Andrew Parish

Surveyed on September 11, 1756   Plat Book C, page 322
Granted on February 5, 1757   Grant Book A, page 418

500 acres bounded on the northeast by John Dehonieur and on all other sides by vacant land. The plat says this is in St. Andrew Parish, although the grant says District of Newport.

****

Stewart, Robert
300 acres in St. Andrew Parish

Granted on December 6, 1757   Grant Book A, page 498

300 acres in the District of Darien and bounded on the north by the South Newport River.

****

Stewart, Robert
300 acres in St. Andrew Parish

Survey date not given   Plat Book C, page 299
Granted on August 6, 1765   Grant Book E, page 199

300 acres formerly laid out for Robert Stewart and by him mortgaged to Grey Elliott and John Gordon. 300 acres bounded on the northwest by the South Newport River. Elapsed and recertified to Grey Elliott and John Gordon on April 3, 1764. Surveyed for Robert Stewart and granted to Grey Elliott and John Gordon.

Stokes, Anthony
350 acres in St. Andrew Parish

Surveyed on July 29, 1771   Plat Book C, page 380
Granted on July 7, 1772   Grant Book I, page 659

350 acres bounded on the east by the old line of survey and
south by Joseph Gibbons. The plat of survey states that this
was granted to Anthony Stokes, now the property of Alexander
Thompson.

****

Stuart, Allan and Stuart, Ann
500 acres in St. Andrew Parish

Granted on July 5, 1774   Grant Book M, page 122

500 acres bounded on all sides by vacant land.

****

Stuart, Allan and Stuart, Ann
300 acres in St. Andrew Parish

Granted on June 6, 1775   Grant Book M, page 1119

300 acres bounded on the southwest by Hugh Ross, John Martin,
Donald McIntosh and James Stewart, north by Elliott and Gordon,
and Joseph Gibbons and northwest by Angus McKay. N. B. This
the last grant made in the Royal Provincial Period.

****

Stuart, Allen
250 acres in St. Andrew Parish

Granted on November 1, 1774   Grant Book M, page 740

250 acres bounded on the south and east by George McIntosh
and on the south by Christopher Rolland.

****

Stuart, Ann and Stuart, Allan
500 acres in St. Andrew Parish

Granted on July 5, 1774   Grant Book M, page 122

500 acres bounded on all sides by vacant land.

****

Stuart, Ann and Stuart, Allan
300 acres in St. Andrew Parish

Granted on June 6, 1775   Grant Book M, page 1119

300 acres bounded on the southwest by Hugh Ross, John Martin, Donald McIntosh and James Stewart, north by Elliott and Gordon and Joseph Gibbons, and on the northwest by Angus McKay. N. B. This is the last Royal Provincial grant in Georgia.

****

Stuart, Ann
250 acres in St. Andrew Parish

Granted on March 7, 1775   Grant Book M, page 1090

250 acres bounded on the southeast by Stephen Drayton.

****

Sullivant, Thomas
400 acres in St. Andrew Parish

Surveyed on May 12, 1768   Plat Book C, page 307
Granted on August 2, 1768   Grant Book G, page 165

400 acres bounded on the northwest by Stephen Williams. The plat shows bounded on the southeast by Grey Elliott.

****

Sullivant, Thomas
100 acres in St. Andrew Parish

Granted on January 3, 1775   Grant Book M, page 931

100 acres bounded on the southeast by William Gibbons, northwest by Jacob Lewis, northeast by Richard Cooper and southwest by White Outerbridge and Smith.

****

Taylor, William
300 acres in St. Andrew Parish

Surveyed on March 10, 1762   Plat Book C, page 360

300 acres bounded on the southwest by the Altamaha River,
northwest by William Herbert, northeast by Marmeduke Perry,
George Moore, Samuel Lewis and Samuel Tomlinson.

****

Telfair, William
500 acres in St. Andrew Parish

Surveyed on August 25, 1771   Plat Book C, page 376
Granted on May 5, 1772   Grant Book I, page 608

500 acres bounded on all sides by vacant land.

****

Thompson, Alexander
300 acres in St. Andrew Parish

Surveyed on January 24, 1772   Plat Book C, page 379
Granted on July 7, 1772   Grant Book I, page 664

300 acres bounded on the northwest by Anthony Stokes, southeast
by land surveyed for Collin Riddock and southwest by the
Altamaha River.

****

Thompson, Alexander
350 acres in St. Andrew Parish

Surveyed on July 29, 1771   Plat Book C, page 380
Granted on July 7, 1772   Grant Book I, page 659

350 acres bounded on the east by the old line of survey,
south by Joseph Gibbons. Plats states that this was granted
to Anthony Stokes, now the property of Alexander Thompson.

****

Thomson, Alexander
150 acres in St. Andrew Parish

Surveyed on October 15, 1772   Plat Book C, page 380
Granted on March 2, 1773   Grant Book I, page 923A

150 acres bounded on the northwest by Anthony Stokes and on
the southwest by the said grantee. Surveyed as Alexander
Thompson.

****

Thornton, Samuel
150 acres in St. Andrew Parish

Surveyed on October 10, 1770   Plat Book C, page 374

150 acres bounded on the west by William Jones, south by
Jonathon Anderson and east by salt marsh.

****

Thornton, Samuel
150 acres in St. Andrew Parish

Surveyed on August 20, 1771   Plat Book C, page 379

150 acres bounded on the southwest by Donald McDonald, northwest by land granted to William Byan and south, southeast
and east by Bruro River and salt marsh.

****

Threadcraft, Thomas
405 acres in St. Andrew Parish

Granted on August 2, 1774   Grant Book M, page 199

405 acres bounded on the northeast by William McIntosh, south
by John Houstoun and Robert McKay. The 405 acres is the
surplus of two tracts; one of 200 acres originally granted
Thomas Threadcraft, the surplus of which is 180¼ acres.
The other tract granted to Abigail Minis, for 500 acres, the
surplus of which was 224 3/4 acres. The 405 acre tract was
granted to John Houstoun.

****

Threadercroft, George
200 acres in St. Andrew Parish

Surveyed on July 28, 1758   Plat Book C, page 361
Granted on December 4, 1759   Grant Book B, page 369

200 acres bounded on the south by Abigail Minis. Surveyed as
George Threadcraft.

****

Todd, John
150 acres in St. Andrew Parish

Surveyed on October 1, 1767   Plat Book C, page 362
Granted on December 1, 1767   Grant Book F, page 431

150 acres bounded on the west by William Forbes, and on the
north by salt marsh.

****

Todd, John
200 acres in St. Andrew Parish

Surveyed on April 14, 1757   Plat Book C, page 362
Granted on March 3, 1767   Grant Book F, page 127

200 acres originally surveyed for John Todd on April 14, 1757,
thence ordered to John Laghteston on September 2, 1766.
Granted to John Lightonston.

****

Tomlinson, Samuel
250 acres in St. Andrew Parish

Surveyed on December 27, 1760   Plat Book C, page 361
Granted on April 13, 1761   Grant Book D, page 74

250 acres bounded on the southeast by land granted George
Moore.

****

Truan, David
500 acres in St. Andrew Parish

Granted on May 5, 1772   Grant Book I, page 609

500 acres bounded on the north by Jane Bourquin.

****

Valloton, David Moses
200 acres in St. Andrew Parish

Granted on November 1, 1774   Grant Book M, page 750

200 acres bounded on all sides by vacant land.

****

Volloton, Jeremiah
100 acres in St. Andrew Parish

Granted on October 4, 1774   Grant Book M, page 607

100 acres bounded on the southwest by Carks and vacant land.

****

Waters, Lamar
300 acres in St. Andrew Parish

Surveyed on May 21, 1770   Plat Book C, page 415

300 acres bounded on the east by David Dicks and north by
John Oates. Surveyed for John Oates in trust for Lamar Waters.

****

Way, Joseph
200 acres in St. Andrew and St. John Parishes

Granted on July 5, 1774   Grant Book M, page 141

200 acres bounded on the west by Jacob Lewis, south by Samuel
Hasting's estate and vacant land, east by William Dunham's
estate and vacant land and north by Joseph Way.

****

Way, Moses
150 acres in St. Andrew Parish

Granted on July 7, 1761   Grant Book C, page 130

150 acres bounded on all sides by vacant land.

****

Way, Moses
200 acres in St. Andrew Parish

Granted on February 7, 1769   Grant Book G, page 275

200 acres bounded on all sides by vacant land.

****

Way, Moses
150 acres in St. Andrew Parish

Granted on April 2, 1771   Grant Book I, page 296·

150 acres bounded partly on the west and partly on the north
by land of the said grantee, and on all other sides vacant.

****

Way, Moses
150 acres in St. Andrew Parish

Granted on January 5, 1773   Grant Book I, page 838

150 acres bounded on all sides by vacant land.

****

Weatherspoon, David
400 acres in St. Andrew Parish

Surveyed on April 1, 1760   Plat Book C, page 433
Granted on May 21, 1762   Grant Book D, page 119

400 acres bounded on the east by Samuel Fulton and John
McClelland, south by Lewis Creek and west by Thomas King.
Surveyed as being the same as above without Lewis Creek.

****

Weech, George
300 acres in St. Andrew Parish

Granted on September 6, 1774   Grant Book M, page 388

300 acres bounded on the southwest by John Patton

****

Wereat, John
360 acres in St. Andrew Parish

Granted on July 7, 1761   Grant Book D, page 63

360 acres bounded on every side by the Altamaha River and a
creek called Rutherford's Creek, the same being an island
situate in the Altamaha River.

                         ****

West, Charles
600 acres in St. Andrew Parish

Granted on November 1, 1774   Grant Book M, page 755

600 acres bounded on the north by Abraham Williams and vacant
land, east by George Gray, southwest by Simon Munro and
vacant land and west by Grey Elliott.

                         ****

Westley, James
150 acres in St. Andrew Parish

Granted on August 4, 1767   Grant Book F, page 334

150 acres including a tract of 100 acres heretofore ordered
to and surveyed for the said James Westley and bounded on
the northeast by Donald McKay and on the southeast by
Norman McDonald.

                         ****

Westly, James
200 acres in St. Andrew Parish

Granted on December 4, 1759   Grant Book B, page 371

200 acres bounded on the north by marsh land vacant, west by
the five acre lots of Darien and south and east by the
Altamaha River.

                         ****

Wetherspoon, John
100 acres in St. Andrew Parish

Granted on March 6, 1764   Grant Book D, page 400

100 acres bounded on the west by Thomas King, south by David Weatherspoon and east by Samuel Fulton.

****

Wetherspoon, John
100 acres in St. Andrew Parish

Granted on September 1, 1767   Grant Book F, page 369

100 acres bounded on the south by _____, west by John Jones and north by George Davis.

****

Williams, Abraham
1000 acres in St. Andrew Parish

Granted on September 1, 1767   Grant Book F, page 371

1000 acres bounded on the north by a small creek and salt marshes.

****

Williams, John
500 acres in St. Andrew Parish

Granted on July 7, 1761   Grant Book C, page 325

500 acres bounded on the south by John Todd, Sr. and John Todd, Jr. and north by the marshes of Newport River.

****

Williams, John Francis
500 acres in St. Andrew Parish

Granted on August 6, 1771   Grant Book I, page 397

500 acres bounded on the east by David Dish, partly on the north by John Oates, partly on the south by some person unknown and on the west by vacant land.

****

Williams, Stephen
100 acres in St. Andrew Parish

Granted on December 3, 1760   Grant Book C, page 49

100 acres bounded on the northwest by the said Stephen Williams.

****

Williams, Stephen

150 acres in St. Andrew Parish

Granted on August 2, 1774   Grant Book M, page 268

150 acres bounded on the southwest by Palmer Golde n and vacant
land, northwest by Lewis Mattier and vacant land, northeast
by Mr. Miller and Robert Burton and southeast by Mr. Maybank.

****

Williams, Stephen; Stewart, John; Baker, Richard, in trust
245 acres in St. Andrew Parish

Granted on July 7, 1772   Grant Book I, page 656

245 acres bounded on the south by the Altamaha River, east
by Rutherford's Creek, north by Lewis' Creek and west by a
creek called the Thoroughfare, and in trust for the heirs
of Charles West, deceased.

****

Williams, William
100 acres in St. Andrew Parish

Granted on April 3, 1770   Grant Book G, page 586A & 586B

100 acres bounded on the southeast by Thomas Peacock.

****

Williams, William
100 acres in St. Andrew Parish

Granted April 3, 1770   Grant Book G, page 589

100 acres bounded on the south by Thomas Peacock.

****

Williams, William
200 acres in St. Andrew Parish

Granted on September 3, 1771   Grant Book I, page 420

200 acres bounded on the southwest by the Altamaha River
and on the northeast by land of William and John Middleton.

****

Williams, William
300 acres in St. Andrew Parish

Granted on September 3, 1771   Grant Book I, page 422

300 acres bounded on the southeast by Matthew Frederick and
northwest by John Middleton.

****

Williamson, Richard
200 acres in St. Andrew Parish

Granted on May 1, 1770   Grant Book I, page 13

200 acres bounded on the southeast by the said Richard
Williamson.

****

Williamson, Richard
1000 acres in St. Andrew Parish

Granted on June 5, 1770   Grant Book I, page 36

1000 acres bounded on the southeast by Samuel Miller.

****

Wilson, John
50 acres in St. Andrew Parish

Granted on February 2, 1773   Grant Book H, page 99

50 acres on bounty and bounded on the east by Button Gwinnett.

****

Winn, John
150 acres in St. Andrew Parish

Granted on October 3, 1769   Grant Book G, page 446

150 acres bounded on the north by Lydia Sanders, east by Joseph Oswell and vacant land, south by Francis Arthur and west by James Andrews.

****

Winn, John
150 acres in St. Andrew Parish

Granted on October 3, 1769   Grant Book G, page 447

150 acres bounded on the east by Lydia Sanders and south by James Andrews.

****

Winn, John
250 acres in St. Andrew Parish

Granted on December 5, 1769   Grant Book G, page 485

250 acres bounded on all sides by vacant land.

****

Winn, John
350 acres in St. Andrew Parish

Granted on October 6, 1772   Grant Book I, page 767

350 acres in trust bounded on all sides by vacant land.

****

Winn, John
150 acres in St. Andrew Parish

Granted on October 6, 1772   Grant Book I, page 771

150 acres bounded on all sides by vacant land.

****

Winn, John
300 acres in St. Andrew Parish

Granted on February 7, 1775   Grant Book M, page 1054

300 acres bounded on the north and south by vacant land, east by John Shute and west by Thomas Golding.

****

Winn, John, Jr.
200 acres in St. Andrew Parish

Granted on November 6, 1770   Grant Book I, page 193

200 acres bounded partly on the southeast and northwest by Thomas Kelly and on all other sides by vacant land.

****

Winn, John, Jr.
100 acres in St. Andrew Parish

Granted on March 2, 1773   Grant Book I, page 924

100 acres bounded on the east by the said grantee.

****

Witherspoon, David
200 acres in St. Andrew Parish

Granted on May 5, 1772   Grant Book I, page 612

200 acres bounded on the south by the said grantee, partly on the west by Robert Baillie and part vacant land, partly on the east by Peter Sallens and part vacant land and on all other sides by land vacnat.

****

Witherspoon, John
150 acres in St. Andrew Parish

Granted on November 1, 1774   Grant Book M, page 757

150 acres bounded on the west by said John Witherspoon, south by _____McLoud and west and north by William Bennet.

****

Woodland, James
200 acres in St. Andrew Parish

Surveyed on May 12, 1759   Plat Book C, page 441
Granted on June 5, 1759   Grant Book B, page 126

200 acres including an island situate on Cedar Point between Darien and Sapelo.

****

Woodland, James
200 acres in St. Andrew Parish

Granted on September 2, 1766   Grant Book E, page 376

200 acres bounded on the west by the Altamaha River and north by Jonathon Woodland.

****

Woodland, James
100 acres in St. Andrew Parish

Granted on June 7, 1768   Grant Book G, page 129

100 acres bounded on all sides by vacant land.

****

Woodland, Jonathon
100 acres in St. Andrew Parish

Granted on June 5, 1764   Grant Book E, page 17

100 acres bounded on the west by the Altamaha River and south by James Woodland.

****

Woodland, Jonathon
150 acres in St. Andrew Parish

Granted on October 29, 1765   Grant Book E, page 312

150 acres bounded on the south by salt marshes of the Altamaha River and on the east by Alexander McKithen.

****

Woodland, William
250 acres in St. Andrew Parish

Granted on October 6, 1767   Grant Book F, page 396

250 acres bounded on the east by John Smith and on the southwest by John Perkins.

****

Woodruffe, Joseph
500 acres in St. Andrew Parish

Granted on July 2, 1771   Grant Book I, page 377

500 acres bounded on the northwest by Clement Martin.

****

Wright, James
2075 acres in St. Andrew Parish

Surveyed on July 1, 1761   Plat Book C, page 432
Granted on November 3, 1761   Grant Book C, page 254

2075 being two islands situate and being in the Altamaha
River and bounded on the south by islands granted to Captain
Raymond Demere and Colonel Mark Carr and land known by the
name of New Hanover, on the north by an island and land
granted Francis Goffe, Thomas Camber and Lachlan McIntosh.

****

Wright, James
100 acres in St. Andrew Parish

Granted on July 5, 1768   Grant Book G, page 144

100 acres bounded on the northwest by Darien Town Common,
southwest by land ordered the said James Wright.

****

Wright, James
44 acres in St. Andrew Parish

Granted on July 5, 1768   Grant Book H, page 10

44 acres being a part of 10 Garden Lots of land to the east of Darien numbered from 1 to 10 and bounded on the north- west by the Town Common of Darien and on the south by Jonathon Bryan.

****

Wright, James
87 acres in St. Andrew Parish

Granted on March 7, 1769   Grant Book H, page 18

87 acres bounded on the west by lands granted James McCulloch, north by land granted Captain John Gray, late of His Majesty's Independent Companies, east by land granted Samuel Fulton and south by Benjamin Lewis.

****

Wright, William
100 acres in St. Andrew Parish

Surveyed on January 30, 1760   Plat Book C, page 433

100 acres bounded on the east by William Davis and south by a marsh.

****

Wylly, Alexander and Johnson, Lewis
150 acres in St. Andrew Parish

Surveyed on March 11, 1761   Plat Book C, page 320
Granted on January 19, 1773   Grant Book I, page 860

150 acres bounded on the southwest by the Altamaha River, and originally surveyed for Samuel Sanders, thence ordered to Lewis Johnson and Alexander Wylly on June 2, 1772. Granted to Johnson and Wylly.

****

Yonge, Henry
400 acres in St. Andrew Parish

Surveyed on March 13, 1773   Plat Book M, page 22
Granted on November 1, 1774   Grant Book M, page 761

400 acres bounded on all sides by vacant land.

Young, Thomas
500 acres in St. Andrew Parish

Granted on July 5, 1774   Grant Book M, page 149

500 acres bounded on the northwest by Robert Miller, southwest by the Altamaha River and southeast by John Dawson.

****

Young, Thomas
660 acres in St. Andrew Parish

Granted on July 5, 1772   Grant Book I, page 614

660 acres bounded on the west by John McClelland and James
McClelland, north by Isaac Lyons, partly on the east by
Samuel Fulton and south by land vacant at the time of the
survey.

****

Young, Thomas
267 acres in St. Andrew Parish

Granted on January 3, 1775   Grant Book M, page 970

267 acres situate on Lewis' Island in the Altamaha River.

****
****
**